Cotters and Squatters

Cotters and Squatters:

Housing's
Hidden History

Colin Ward

Five Leaves Publications
www.fiveleaves.co.uk

Cotters and Squatters:
Housing's Hidden History
by Colin Ward

Published in 2002, reprinted in 2005 by Five Leaves,
PO Box 81, Nottingham NG5 4ER
www.fiveleaves.co.uk

The cover illustration is taken from Oscar Zarate's poster
for the film *Winstanley*, and is used
by permission of the artist.

Five Leaves acknowledges financial assistance
from East Midlands Arts

Typeset by 4 Sheets Design & Print Ltd.
Printed in Great Britain

By the Same Author

*Published by Five Leaves
+Forthcoming Five Leaves edition

Asses, swine, have litter spread,
and with fitting food are fed,
All things have a home but one —
Thou, Oh Englishman hast none!

Shelley

Contents

Foreword and acknowledgements

At the end of the second world war I reported, in the anarchist paper *Freedom*, on the occupation of military camps by homeless families, and became aware that these people adopting direct action to solve an immediate practical problem were part of an ancient tradition that I knew nothing about.[1] When the squatters' campaign emerged again in the 1960s, I was gratified that the London Squatters thought it useful to reprint my reports of 1946, and over the years I wrote at great length about radical approaches to housing issues. When Nick Wates and Christian Wolmar produced the richly illustrated book *Squatting: the real story* in 1980, it fell to me to contribute the chapter which, however inadequately, described the period from the Middle Ages to the inter-war years.[2]

I was aware that there was a history to be explored, but the opportunities that came my way were for the examination of quite different aspects of popular and unofficial environments. I had a marvellous time tracing the evolution of the Plotlands and the origins of holiday camps with Dennis Hardy, and the history and culture of allotment gardens with David Crouch, thanks to grants from the bodies that fund the bed-and-breakfast charges and rail fares involved in pursuing research.[3] But none could be persuaded to help me explore the hidden history of squatter housing.

However, if I could not produce the scholarly book that the topic demands, I could at least produce a book, thanks to the help that flowed in whenever I talked about this theme, from the annual conference of the Museum Association at Plymouth and that of Shelter at Nottingham, to that of the Oral History Society at Brighton. The community of scholars really exists, and people have been eager to offer me nuggets of information to incorporate in this book, and to persuade us that the place of the squatter in the history of housing and in that of both agriculture and industry, has been more significant than we realised.

The backbone of this book has been the work of a series of regional researchers, most of it sadly inaccessible to the ordinary reader. For Chapters 4 and 5 on Wales, I am immensely indebted to Roger Laidlaw. For Chapter 6 on South-west England, I drew upon the continuing work of the Somerset and South Avon Vernacular Building Research Group, which will, I hope, slowly work its meticulous way across the county. For Chapter 8 on Herefordshire, I am grateful for the wonderfully detailed dissertation by James Moir, who was also my guide in attempts to unravel the folklore of the one-night house.

For Chapter 9, on the role of squatter housing at the birthplaces of industry, I have been privileged to see Barrie Trinder at work with students in Shropshire in the 1970s and Andrew Dobraszczyc at work with his in Staffordshire in the 1990s, and to benefit from their research. For Chapter 10 it was a delight to draw upon the work of Raphael Samuel who, for years, urged me to get this book compiled before it was too late. Alas, it was compiled too late for him to tell me what is missing.

Readers of Anthony Trollope's *The Last Chronicle of Barset* (1867) will feel on familiar ground in Chapters 9 and 10. For his account of the colony of brickmakers which had sprung up on the canal banks, far from the centre of the village of Hogglestock, is close to historical truth. His central figure, the poor parson Josiah Crawley, ministered to the families who were hated by the farmers and vilified by the tradesmen. Trollope comments, as do the historians, that "They got drunk occasionally, but I doubt if they drank more than did the farmers themselves on market-day... That they worked very hard was certain; and it was certain also that very few of their number ever came upon the poor rates."

The Scottish experience, with a different history of land tenure, is scarcely described here, except for the account in Chapter 2 of the evicted poor who had to resort to cave-dwelling, both in their own ancestral land and on deportation to Canada, and in Chapter 12, where the minimal distinction between 'cottars' and 'squatters' in the Highlands and Islands is cited.

For chance conversations about vernacular buildings, spread over forty years and between London, Devon and Oxford, I have been greatly indebted to Paul Oliver, and in gathering facts about caves I was helped by Lee Wright of Leeds, Mary Ward of Worcester and Ross Bradshaw of Nottingham. For other nuggets of vital information I am grateful to Paul Coones, Jennifer Culpin, Griffiths Cunningham, Mary Gryspeerdt, Alun Howkins, Bob Jones, Steve Platt, Brian Richardson, Brian Short and Peter Sparkes.

I have a lifelong debt to public library services everywhere, with special thanks to Geoff Ross of Hadleigh Library, to Richard Shackle of Colchester Local History Library, and to the staff of several County Record Offices.

I am very grateful to the New Forest Museum and Visitor Centre, the West Country Studies Library, Leicester University Press, the Ironbridge Gorge Museum Trust, as well as to Paul Coones and Peter Jones, and the late Raphael Samuel for the use of their photographs, and to Oscar Zarate who provided the cover illustration. I have a special debt to friends who took photographs especially for this book: Jenny Gould, Ian Bailey and Lee Wright.

1. My reports from *Freedom* in 1946 were reprinted in *Anarchy* 23, Vol 3 No 1, January 1963 pp. 9-15, reprinted as a pamphlet by the London Squatters 1969, and in Colin Ward *Housing: an anarchist approach*, London: Freedom Press 1976, 1983 pp. 19-27.
2. Colin Ward "The Early Squatters" in Nick Wates and Christian Wolmar (eds) *Squatting: the real story*, London: Bay Leaf Books 1980 pp. 104-109.
3. Dennis Hardy & Colin Ward *Arcadia for All: the legacy of a makeshift landscape*, London: Mansell 1984, and *Goodnight Campers: The history of the British holiday camp*, London: Mansell 1986. David Crouch & Colin Ward: *The Allotment: its landscape and culture*, London: Faber 1988, Nottingham: Five Leaves.

Harry Burt, A New Forest Commoner, outside his holding c.1950.
(PHOTO: NEW FOREST MUSEUM AND VISITOR CENTRE).

Chapter 1
The global one-night house

"It was a notion held among the peasantry in olden times, that he who could in one night erect a 'Mushroom Hall' or a 'now-or-never', without hindrance from the officials of the manor, had obtained a copyhold right to the land."

Richard Heath *The English Peasant*[1]

There is a belief around the world that if you can build a house between sunset and sunrise, then the owner of the land cannot expel you. There are many variations on this theme. The condition might be that the roof is in place, or that a pot is boiling on the fire, or that smoke can be seen emerging from the chimney. This last stipulation seems an impossible result of a single night's work, and it led me to wonder if the story was simply an account of events that could not really happen, like Birnam Wood's transplantation to Dunsinane.

Could this belief belong to the realm of fairy tale descriptions of the impossible, like Jack's fast-growing overnight bean-stalk? But collectors of fairy stories from many countries were unable to help me find one depending upon the magic of overnight house-building. Yet it is remarkable how, if you visit villages in many parts of rural Britain, your hosts will draw attention to a particular cottage, sometimes long and narrow and close to the roadside, but sometimes eccentrically sited on the village green, and will explain that it was said to be a squatter house, originally built in a night.

Sometimes searches into manor court rolls in the county record office show that the legend is well-founded and that the building of the cottage may have been legitimised by local definitions of "squatters' rights" or regularised by the imposition of annual fines which became converted into rents or, eventually, to freehold tenure.

The concept of the one-night house has an astonishing global distribution, sometimes as folklore, sometimes, it is said, as customary law, or even as statutory law. For example, in the self-organised invasions of land on the fringe of the cities of Latin America in the latter half of the 20th century, the occupation of the chosen site takes place once darkness has fallen, and token walls of straw matting or corrugated sheeting are erected. Sometimes, according to the whims of the ruling regimes, the police swoop in the morning, in which case another later invasion happens, and another, until the settlers are left in peace. Eeventually, the dwelling is given a roof, as John Turner noted, "a common and heartening scene in villages and squatter settlements throughout Peru is the celebration of roofing a house, a ritual occasion that brings family and friends together."[2]

Novelists and film-makers love the folklore of the one-night house for its dramatic possibilities, and they enjoy especially the symbolism of the local community pooling its efforts to provide a house for a new couple, celebrating not only the formation of a new family but the goodwill and solidarity of the village or neighbourhood. Thus the Cumbrian poet Robert Anderson (while forgetting the fact that clay or mud walls have to be built in stages and allowed to dry out), joyfully described the festive atmosphere of the construction of an earthen-walled house at the end of the 18th century:

"That everything might be done in order, and without confusion, a particular piece of work is assigned to each labourer. Some dig the clay, some fetch it in wheelbarrows, some heave it upon the walls. The rustic girls (a great many of which attend on the occasion), fetch the water with which the clay is softened, from some neighbouring ditch or pond. When the walls are raised to their proper height, the

6

company have plenty to eat and drink: after which the lads and lasses, with faces incrusted with clay and dirt, take a dance upon the clay-floor of the newly-erected cottage."[3]

The Italian version of the folk-lore of the one-night house was the subject of Vittorio De Sica's film *Il Tetto* (The Roof) which appeared in 1956. The script was written by Cesare Zavattini, who based it on the experiences of a couple expecting their first child, whose income was not enough to buy them shelter, and who decided to build a hut in a settlement called Val Melaina. Apart from the use of their own labour, a builder specialising in clandestine building would have to be employed, and the materials would have to be purchased in advance.

Zavattini suggested to Rossellini that a film company should pay the cost of the materials, (about 60,000 lire at that time), in return for the right to film the operation. This proposal came to nothing, but Zavattini pursued the idea with Vittorio De Sica and eventually they made the film.

Michele Gandin's account of the making of the film provides us with details of the illicit house-building sector of the 1950s in northern Italy. Apparently, if the police arrived before the roof was laid, the builder was subject to heavy fines, and the building would be demolished. If the roof was there and the building occupied, security had been won. It became a matter for the endlessly protracted procedures of the civil courts, usually sympathetic to the plight of the young couple and their child. The convention of building in the hours of darkness with concrete blocks and cement-and-lime mortar, with no time allowed for the structure to dry out in stages, added to the difficulties and disappointments of this method, but also to the drama of the film.[4]

A more recent film, *La estrategia del caracol* (The Snail's Strategy) made in Colombia in 1993, seeks to dramatise the belief that its director, Sergio Cabrera, describes as a remnant from ancient Germanic law, claiming that so long as there is no trace of a break-in to the site and that it is furnished with a table and four chairs, a house built in one night, if it has a roof, cannot be torn down.[5]

In eastern France, a scholar, G. Jeanton, from the Bresse region around Macon, described how it was generally understood there that every individual had a right to appropriate a portion of the commune's land and to build a house between sunset and sunrise. If the house was finished by dawn, the constructor's right to the land was recognised by local custom, and "up to the present time (1923) none of the communes seem to have disputed that right." He explained how the younger members of poor families would sometimes spend the whole winter preparing the woodwork of their house with their parents and friends. On a fine night when all was ready, the family would assemble on a patch of waste land, and with great agility would erect the house "rustic, no doubt, but complete from its wooden threshold to its thatched roof," and "when the sun rose, its rays would shine on the bunch of flowers that the peasant architects had placed at the top of the roof."[6]

Writing many years later, in 1939, Jeanton explained that a man who already had a house could not claim the right to build a one-night house, that the house could be inherited by descendants, that if it were sold the commune had to be compensated for the value of the ground, and that sometimes a small rent was payable to the commune. The legal position was uncertain, despite the Civil Code and a battery of lawyers. In some districts a man who wanted to build could apply to the commune and be granted permission without the obligation to build in one night.

It had been suggested that this right was a survival from Roman Law, but Jeanton remarks that the same custom is found in Cornwall where Roman Law had not applied. He suggests that it is more likely to derive from ancient Indo-European folklore.[7]

Turkey has a similar long tradition of recognition for a particular special status for the house built between sunset and sunrise. A long time ago the authors of a study of global housing issues explained that "In Turkey, where perhaps half of Ankara's 1.5 millions live this way, there are *gecekondu* — acknowledging the fact that, to avoid instant legal destruction, any temporary dwelling has to be erected in a single night between dusk and dawn."[8] Their most recent admirer is the philosopher Roger Scruton who sees the contemporary *gecekondu* as "the happiest example of modern urbanisation that I know", and explains that, "These grew up as a result of an old Ottoman law which contains all the wisdom that a city needs. According to this law (the validity of which has never been tested), anyone who finds a plot of land that is neither owned nor used can establish title to it, on condition that he erects a dwelling there in the space of a night (*gece* = night; *kondurmak* = to find lodgings). The result is a miracle of harmonious settlement: houses of one or two storeys, in easily handled materials such as brick, wood and tiles, nestling close together, since none can lay claim to any more garden than the corners left over from building, each fitted neatly into the hillside, and with tracks running among them through which no cars can pass. In time the residents cover them with stucco and paint them in those lovely Turkish blues and ochres; they bring electricity and water, they light their little paths not with glaring sodium lights but with intermittent bulbs, twinkling from afar like grounded galaxies."[9]

Similarly, in the case of squatter settlements in Latin America, favourable circumstances can enable those overnight adventurers to form communities that evolve in about fifteen years into fully-serviced suburbs, providing livelihoods as well as homes, through people's ability to turn their labour into capital. This is something that neither government nor the market economy can do for the least influential of citizens.

The British equivalent of belief in the special qualities of the one-night house is explored in the chapters that follow. It has survived best in the memories and folk-lore of the Welsh, as can be gathered from chapters 4 and 5. One of those who celebrated it, particularly in the context of friends and neighbours building a nest for a newly-espoused couple was the Welsh author Hugh Evans who described how he had never met a happier-looking woman than Ellen Richards, who had reared six children in her turf cottage, with its peat fire. "The poor cottage was her castle," he remembered, "and love transmuted everything into gold." Lest we should accuse him of sentimentality, he described the way she had managed, and explained that:

> "The *caban unnos*, a squatter's cottage of turf, is a hut built in one night, hence the name. If a man put up a cottage between sunset and sunrise and if he lit a fire on the hearth and sent smoke through a chimney, it was a recognised custom that he might remain in possession of the house although it was built on common land. Sometimes this happened when a bachelor took it into his head to get married and to set up house. His friends would gather at twilight and work all night to construct the turf hut; it was one of the conditions that the house should be complete with the chimney smoking before sunrise the next morning, and if there was time and labour enough a turf wall would be raised to enclose a garden. Hundreds of such houses were built, and hundreds were filched from the rightful owners by the schemes and trickery of the landowners."[10]

The intriguingly widespread folklore of the one-night house seems to be an attempt to find a loophole in the stranglehold of land-ownership to create an opportunity to change a family's destiny. And the fact that the examples I have cited of this tradition attribute its origins almost at random to old Germanic law, Roman law, old Ottoman law and Indo-European tradition, show very clearly that nobody knows where this ancient subversive legend came from, but that we all have an interest in claiming its legitimacy.

Peter Sparkes of the Faculty of Law at Southampton kindly suggested to me the links between the different legal traditions I had mentioned, speculating that "the universality of this supposed custom must mean that it derives either from Roman law (Ottoman law is Roman law as applied to the eastern empire) or from Germanic custom. Roman law basically applied to the south-western parts of Europe and Germanic custom to the north-eastern parts. The case you discuss at Macon is interesting because in pre-revolutionary France this lay just about on the border between the two laws..."[11]

No authority I have consulted, however, suggests any legislation or example in case law that refers to this belief. All the same, in many human societies there is a belief that access to land, regardless of the kings, conquerors, robber barons or bureaucrats of the past, must be a natural right for the current generation of humanity. This was beautifully expressed in the 18th century by Thomas Spence in a work with a memorable title. It is: "A Lecture read at the Philosophical Society in Newcastle on November 8th, 1775, for Printing of which the Society did the Author the Honour to expel him."[12]

Spence explained to his audience that the first landholders were usurpers, and tyrants over "poor dependent needy wretches" and that the same must apply to those who have since possessed the land by inheritance or purchase,

> "...And any of them still can, by laws of their own making, oblige every living creature to remove off his property (which, to the great distress of mankind, is too often put in execution); so of consequence were all the landholders to be of one mind, and determined to take their properties into their

own hands, all the rest of mankind might go to heaven if they would, for there would be no place found for them here."[13]

The Highland Clearances in Scotland were an immediate illustration of the point he was making, as were the side-effects of Enclosure in England. Over a century before Spence, Gerrard Winstanley declared that "the poorest man hath as true a title and just right to the land as the richest man." He held the view, widespread among the radicals of his day, that it was the Norman Conquest which had deprived the people of their land, and that with the deposition of Charles I, the ultimate heir of William I, the people had won back the land by the same right of conquest. He thus added the argument of a legal title to that of a natural right.

Many cultures around the world have a traditional belief that the land is naturally the common property of the people. "The landlord owns the peasants but the peasants own the land" is a Russian saying from the days when the rich measured their wealth in 'souls'. In England and Wales, most people assume that the pathetic remnants of the common land are in fact common property. This belief itself can be seen as a precious survival of ancient popular wisdom. For in legal fact, as the historians of the commons explain, "all common land is private property. It belongs to someone, whether an individual or a corporation, and has done so from time immemorial." But they go on to conclude that

"Common rights were not something specifically granted by a generous landlord, but were the residue of rights that were once more extensive, rights that in all probability antedate the idea of private property in land, and are therefore of vast antiquity.[14]

And in all probability, so too is the belief that, despite the claim by the powerful to be monarchs of all they survey, the poor and homeless can, overnight, win a place in the sun.

References

1. Richard Heath *The English Peasant,* London: Fisher Unwin 1893 p.87
2. John Turner "The Re-education of a Professional" in John F.C. Turner and Robert Fichter (eds) *Freedom to Build,* New York: Macmillan 1972 p.133.
3. Robert Anderson, cited in Anthony Quiney *Wall to Wall,* London: BBC Publications 1994.
4. Michele Gandin (ed) *Il Tetto di Vittorio De Sica,* Milano: Cappelli Editore 1956 pp. 29 and 53.
5. *La estrategia del caracol* (1993), directed by Sergio Cabrera. (Information from Francesca Leita of Centro Espressioni Cinematographiche, Udine).
6. G. Jeanton in *Maconnais Traditionaliste et Populaire* Tome IV (1923) cited in 7. below.
7. G. Jeanton "Les maisons construites en une nuit" in *Revue de Folklore Francais* Vol 10 No 2, Avril-Juin 1939 pp. 33-39
8. Peter Wilsher and Rosemary Righter *The Exploding Cities,* London: Andre Deutsch 1975 p.19.
9. Roger Scruton "Under scrutiny" *Perspectives* Issue 32, December 1997/January 1998 p.91. The standard account is Kemal H. Karpat *The Gecekondu: rural migration and urbanization in Turkey,* New York: Cambridge University Press 1976.
10. Hugh Evans (1854-1934) *The Gorse Glen,* trans. from the Welsh by E. Morgan Humphreys, in D.N. and E.N. Lloyd *A Book of Wales,* London: Collins 1953 pp. 153-154.
11. Peter Sparkes, personal communication 26 May 2000.
12. Thomas Spence "A Lecture Read at the Philosophical Society in Newcastle on November 8th 1775, for Printing of which the Society did the author the Honour to expel him." Reprinted in N. Beer (ed) *The Pioneers of Land Reform,* London: G. Bell & Sons 1920
13. *ibid.*
14. W.G. Hoskins and L. Dudley Stamp *The Common Lands of England and Wales,* London: Collins 1963.

Chapter 2
Cave-dwellers in Britain

"Adam and Eve, according to the fable, wore the bower before other clothes. Man wanted a home, a place of warmth, or comfort, first of physical warmth, then the warmth of the affections. We may imagine a time when, in the infancy of the human race, some enterprising mortal crept into a hollow in a rock for shelter. Every child begins the world again, to some extent, and loves to stay outdoors, even in wet and cold. It plays house, as well as horse, having an instinct for it. Who does not remember the interest with which, when young, he looked at shelving rocks, or any approach to a cave?"

Henry David Thoreau *Walden*[1]

No doubt Adam and Eve, building their bower of branches and leaves in the Garden of Eden, were the first squatters, and were subsequently evicted by their landlords, but Kent's Cavern, near Torquay in Devon is the earliest known squatter colony in the British Isles. "In 1989, using the latest scientific techniques, experts established that the cavern was the oldest identified human settlement in Britain, dating back at least 500,000 years... A jawbone discovered in the cavern in 1927 was found by radiocarbon dating to be 31,000 years old, making it the oldest specimen of *Homo sapiens* — or completely modern man — to be found anywhere in Europe."[2] And everywhere, if there are natural cave systems or easily-penetrated stone (or even peat) there is a history, both ancient and modern, of human occupation and squatter settlement.

It was a necessity for the poor people of Kildare, described by the Irish traveller Aidan Higgins who tells how "Less than a century before I was born the bog people of old Kildare were reduced to living underground in the bog itself, from whence the carters with their turf-carts and small donkeys carried loads off to distant Dublin, and came back asleep in their empty carts."[3]

The city of Nottingham grew up around a sandstone hill on which the castle stands, with 40-metre high cliffs overlooking the Trent valley. The bedrock of the city's geology is called Sherwood Sandstone and the advantages are explained by its historian Tony Waltham who tells how "it is easily excavated with only hand tools, yet will safely stand as an unsupported arch of low profile." There are outcrops of this stone elsewhere in the county, at Worksop, Arnold, Cresswell Crags and Mansfield, where Rock Cottage is excavated out of the hillside at the edge of the road. Beneath the city centre in Nottingham there are more then 400 caves, all of them man-made. Tony Waltham explains that "they include caves cut as storerooms, basements, factories, pub cellars, dwelling houses and air-raid shelters, along with a few sand mines; the oldest date back at least 750 years."[4] A traveller in 1639, John Taylor, described how

"a great number of the inhabitants (especially the poorer sort) doe dwell in vallts, holes, or caves, which are cut and digged out (or within) the Rocke: so that if a man be destitute of a house, it is but to goe to Nottingham, and with a Mattock, a Shovell, a Crow of Iron, a Chizell, and Mallet, and sauch instruments, he may play the Mole, the Cunny, or the Pioner, and worke himselfe a Hole, or a Burrow, for him and his family: where, over their heads the grasse and pasture growes, and beasts do feed; faire Orchards and gardens are their coverings, and Cowes are milkt upon the tops of their houses."[5]

Tony Waltham's account explains that paupers lived in caves alongside the three main roads out of Nottingham at various times between the 14th and 19th centuries. On the

Hollow Stone road, originally the main route into town from the south, "Squatters were ejected from the caves in 1607 before the entrances were sealed up, though some caves in the same road were rented to the poor in 1611. But many or all of these caves must have been destroyed when Hollow Stone was widened in 1740, and it is a new generation of caves which were bricked up to discourage vagrants in 1975."[6] By 1998, when the Drury Hill Caves beneath the Broad Marsh shopping centre had been refurbished as a tourist attraction, the city council began sealing off caves below the castle because young homeless people had taken to sleeping there.

The other British city built over man-made caves is the Old Town of Edinburgh. It runs along a ridge of volcanic rock between Holyrood House and the Castle, along what is now known as the High Street or Royal Mile. Parallel to this famous street is another ridge of soft sandstone in which, as the buildings became higher, so, as Jan-Andrew Henderson explains,

> "the foundations became deeper and countless cellars were created. The steep slopes on either side of the High Street meant that these foundations and cellars didn't necessarily have to be excavated from above, builders could dig sideways into the ridge, allowing underground levels to be built at a depth that would not have been possible in any other location... the cellars were more like caves slotted into the hillside."

Cave dwellings were not often the result of sudden emergencies, because of the labour involved. A well-known tourist attraction at Knaresborough in North Yorkshire is the group of houses carved out of the rock face over the river Nidd. One was excavated over the years from 1770 onward by a weaver called Thomas Hill and his son, and it consists of four rooms hollowed out of the limestone. The most recent occupant, Nancy Buckle, belonged to the fifth generation of descendants of the original builder. But, of course, her family could not prove ownership of the land itself, whose present inheritors are the Ampleforth Abbey trustees. In 1994 Ms Buckle was told by the trustees that she must quit her home as it was deemed unfit for human habitation, although it had by that time become a Grade 2 listed building. In the year 2000 the trustees sold the cave to an antique dealer who declared that

> "When it comes to properties of this kind we are only custodians looking after our heritage. I intend to restore it with great care and then perhaps share it by opening it a couple of days a year to people who, like me, are fascinated with history."[8]

At Kinver, not far from Stourbridge in the West Midlands, another sandstone escarpment provided homes for generations of ironworkers and their families. They carved them out, extended them and re-fronted them over many generations. Their houses were approached by way of gardens full of fruit trees and strawberries. This was at Holy Austin Rock below the northern point of Kinver Edge, where twelve families, mostly workers at the Hyde Iron Works, were living in 1901, and six in 1951. The Shaw family were there for more than 150 years. The last resident was Mrs Rose Novak, who lived there from 1949 until the council insisted on rehousing her in 1956. When she left, her house fell victim to vandals but the site has been restored by the National Trust as part of our Heritage. That part of South Staffordshire and North Worcestershire has a series of cave dwellings, hollowed out from the rock and fronted by brick-built extensions. South of Holy Austin Rock, there is Nanny's Rock, and there are more at Drakelow.

When Donna Saker went in search of Worcestershire cave dwellings in 1974 she found that

> "In the villages around Kidderminster, many of them now hidden by brambles and bracken, are

rock-dwellings which have been lived in from medieval times to within living memory. You can still find some of them; and you can go there and see for yourself the hollowed rooms, the rough-cut steps and the remains of the brick 'extensions' which were added probably as recently as the last 40 or 50 years... At Drakelow there are rock cottages, fairytale places half rock, half house; most have been closed and are difficult to find but one has been lived in until this year... At Wolverley you can see a house built partly from the rock on which it stands, and in the cliff near the centre of the village are the dugouts in which a 19th century ironmaster is said to have housed his labourers. Redstone and Blackstone Rocks are two hermitages guarding opposite banks of the Severn near Areley Kings; the caves at Redshone, in a high red cliff by the river, are supposed to have been the hermitage of Layamon, a 12th century priest and poet who wrote an early history of Britain... A little further way, at Stanford-on-Tame, is Southstone Rock..."[9]

Near Astley, about eleven miles north of Worcester, there are caves, also said to have been excavated as a hermitage by monks, which later "passed through a variety of uses, including that of an alehouse and a school, before being turned into six miserable dwellings for very poor families, who had to contend with floods in winter and water oozing from the walls in summer."[10] At Wolverley in August 2000, a pair of cave dwellings, one derelict and the other "reasonably preserved" were put on the market, attracting sixteen bidders and were sold for £30,000.[11]

Another series of inland caves in Britain are the limestone labyrinths of the Mendip Hills and the Cheddar Gorge in Somerset. At the beginning of the 20th century, the pioneer of cave exploration, Herbert Balch of Wells, found that Wookey Hole Cave had been colonised by a Breton tribe in about 250 BC and had been occupied continually for centuries. A caving historian, C.H. Kenney, describes how

> "from time to time, refugees from the community made caves their home, and it seems very likely that legends such as the 'Witch of Wookey' arose in this way. Caves were regarded as places of evil spirits, and anyone who chose to live in a cave no doubt soon became feared as the local witch. A recent example is Nancy Camel's Hole where in the 18th century a woman of that name became a social outcast from the village of Croscombe, and was compelled by circumstances to live in a cave."[12]

The most idyllic evocation of blissful cave-dwelling life comes from the novelist Alan Sillitoe, exploring not his native Nottingham, but the coast of Kent. In 1983 he walked around that coast from Gravesend to Rye, noticing all those places that the guidebooks leave out. But one guidebook feature that he sought in vain as he strode out of Dover was Otter Cottage. This, he had learned from his copy of Murray's 1877 handbook for Kent, was "the Robinson Crusoe-like establishment of an old fisherman called Gatehouse, who with children and grandchildren pursued a variety of avocations, keeping goats, pigs and poultry, and looking out for flotsam and jetsam, and cultivating with success fig trees and vines against the lofty railway embankment." Otter Cottage was another cave carved out of the chalk hillside, and Sillitoe could find no trace of it. He concluded that "Probably the last happy Gatehouse left the locality when schools, taxes and census-takers gleefully wiped out their Eden-like nest."[13]

In the early 18th century, Daniel Defoe, in his account of the Peak District in Derbyshire, described the domestic life of a lead-miner's family living in a cave known as the Giant's Tomb:

"The habitation was poor, 'tis tru, but things within did not look so like misery as I expected. Every thing was clean and neat, tho' mean and ordinary: There were shelves with earthen ware, and some pewter and brass. There was, which I observed in particular, a whole flitch or side of bacon hanging up in the chimney, and by it a good piece of another. There was a sow and pigs running about at the door, and a little lean cow feeding upon a green place, just before the door, and the little enclosed piece of ground I mentioned, was growing with good barley; it being then near harvest."[14]

But most cave-dwellers were less fortunately placed. In 1864, the Relieving Officer for the Chapel-en-le-Frith Poor Law Union wrote to the Registrar General from Derbyshire to describe how

"a number of small excavations have been made into a large hillock of lime ashes (the refuse of lime kilns) which are used as dwellings and occupied by labourers and others employed in the construction through that neighbourhood. The excavations are small, and damp, and have no drains or privies about them and not the slightest means of ventilation except up a hole pulled up through the top, and used for a chimney. In consequence of this defect, smallpox has been raging for some time..."[15]

Before the founding of the National Coal Board in 1947, miners and their families lived in houses rented from the colliery owners. A mineworker who was sacked was simultaneously evicted with his family from the company's housing. Mr John Porter of Peterlee told me how such families were obliged to move into the 'crees', cabins or huts which they had built in their allotment gardens. In the 1930s, 32 families were living like this at Horden while others were reduced to living in caves along the beach between Easington Colliery and Blackhall. (The beach had not yet been polluted by the wholesale tipping of colliery waste).

Scotland provides the most tragic examples of peasants driven to living in caves. The historian T.C. Smout cites an account of the homes of Scottish 'cottars' in 1679. At that time nearly half the population were described by Thomas Kirke as living in

> "such miserable huts as never eye beheld; men women and children pig together in a poor mouse-hole of mud, heath and some such like matter; in some parts where turf is plentiful they build up little cabins thereof with arched roofs of turf without a stick of timber in it; when their houses are dry enough to burn it serves them for fuel and they remove to another."[16]

A century later, "a cottar's house could be run up in a single day if the materials had been gathered beforehand", though by this time it might have stone walls, five foot high, and a timber roof thatched with straw. The valuable roof timbers might move with the cottar to a new site, although "Baron courts laid special penalties on those who took their roof tree with them when they removed from their dwellings."[17]

The Highland peasantry were already living in extreme poverty when their landlords decided that sheep were a more profitable use of land. The most notorious example was the county of Sutherland, where, as Dr Smout explained, between 1807 and 1821,

> "the factors of the Countess of Sutherland and her husband Lord Stafford who owned more than two-thirds of the land in the county expelled from their homes somewhere between five and ten thousand people to make way for sheep."[18]

Other landlords in the Highlands and Islands were pursuing identical aims, providing a living illustration of the ultimate logic of the private monopoly in land that I have quoted from Thomas Spence, the fact that the landlord "can oblige every living creature to remove off his property" so that "were all the landowners to be of one mind, all the rest of mankind might go to heaven if they would, for there would be no place to be found for them here."[19]

Tales are told of desperate people taking refuge on the shore and in caves:

"John McKinnon, a cottar, aged 44, with a wife and six children, had his home pulled down, and had no place to put his head in, consequently he and his family, for the first night or two, had to burrow among the rocks near the shore. When he thought that the factor and his party had left the district, he emerged from the rocks, surveyed the ruins of his former dwelling, saw his furniture and other effects exposed to the elements, and now scarcely worth the lifting."[20]

At Knoydart on the Isle of Skye, "four hundred people were cleared from their homes, and those who refused to go in the boats ran to the hills and hid in caves."[21] At Tarskavaig, one of the villages on Skye where some of the evicted crofters settled in the 1850s, Archie Gilleasbaig related how

"They were piling them into this village, people were living in little huts by the shore. And then they built themselves houses — you could tell them, they all faced north and east and the back wall was the rock."[22]

He was describing his grandmother's experience to David Craig who, in the 1980s travelled through the Highlands and Islands and across Canada to learn what happened to the evicted families. On Barra, at the southernmost tip of the Outer Hebrides, he was told how "the cleared people 'squatted in huts on the foreshore', 'living in crevices on the foreshore', or 'stuck like limpets to a rock.'"[23] However, on Baleshare, a small island north of North Uist, he heard from John McAulay about the landlord of the Sollas estate, an exception, who was described as lenient: "When you wanted a place there, you collected a few friends and built a house at night and put a fire to it."[24] This is one of the few instances of a Scottish reference to the folklore of the one-night house.

In Canada, David Craig was told of family histories, some of which echoed experiences back home. At Glengarry, at the extreme east of Ontario he learned from Marion MacMaster of the adventures of destitute immigrants from South Uist:

> "There were some squatters in Glengarry — little houses here and there. The community took on responsibility for them, they were given milk and tea — some would get a cow presently... My husband tells of a lady they called Cailleach (old woman) Fawcett, way back in the bush, away from the society of the time. One day she was at church — the landowner burned her house. Didn't need the land — just did it out of spite or impatience..."[25]

But elsewhere the more typical response was of relief. In Manitoba, despite their epic of endurance in finding their feet as farmers, the earliest settlers were happy to feel "that they were no longer 'tenants at will', but holders of free estate, labouring on their own land, from which no tyrannical landlords could remove them."[26] Living in caves became part of the family folklore to be passed to the grandchildren.

Back home in Scotland, it was reported that after the forcible eviction of a poor tailor and his family from Applecross at the order of the Duchess of Leeds, "The people were warned that if any shelter were given to the family, those involved would also be evicted."[27]

England too provides a few examples of man-made caves as refuges for the victims of enclosure. Near the great loop in the Southern Wye in Herefordshire, there is a cave known as King Arthur's Cave which was inhabited in the Stone Age, and the site of another, now destroyed by quarrying, where

"Slippery Jimmy lived in a much later man-made den some four feet in diameter and seven or eight feet high. He was a victim of enclosure evictions in the 1830s and lived as a hermit in this thickly thatched home for almost 40 years, living off what he could trap and grow."[28]

References
1. Henry David Thoreau *Walden*, (1858) Penguin Illustrated Classics 1938 p.48.
2. Robin Whiteman *The West Country*, London: Weidenfield & Nicolson 1993 p.13.
3. Aidan Higgins *Donkey's Years*, London: Secker & Warburg 1995 p.331.
4. Tony Waltham *Sandstone Caves of Nottingham*, East Midlands Geological Society 1993 p.1 (reprint from *Mercian Geologist* Vol 13, Sept 1992).
5. John Taylor *Part of this Summer's Travels...* (1639) reprint (L 93.01) in Local Studies Library, Nottingham.
6. Waltham *op cit* p.7.
7. Jan-Andrew Henderson *The Town Below the Ground*, Edinburgh: Mainstream 1999 p.20.
8. *Yorkshire Evening Post* 6 December 1993 and 26 May 2000.
9. "Cavemen — ancient and modern" *Worcester Evening News* 28 December 1974.
10. "Rocks of ages have stood the test of time" *Worcester Evening News* 30 January 1999.
11. "Cave is sold" *Barrows' Worcester Journal* 25 August 2000.
12. C.H. Kenney "Mendip Underground" in W.G. Hall (ed) *Man and the Mendips*, Taunton: The Mendip Society 1971.
13. Alan Sillitoe *The Saxon Shoreway*, London: Hutchinson 1983.

14. Daniel Defoe *A Tour Through England and Wales* (1724), London: J.M. Dent 1948 Vol 2 p.162
15. cited in Enid Gauldie *Cruel Habitations: A History of Working-Class Housing 1780-1918*, London: George Allen & Unwin 1974 p.26.
16. cited in T.C. Smout *A History of the Scottish People 1560-1830*, London: Collins 1969 p.150
17. *ibid* p.149.
18. *ibid* p.353.
19. Thomas Spence *op cit.*
20. Alexander MacKenzie *The History of the Highland Clearances* (1883), Edinburgh: Mercat Press 1994 p.272.
21. John Prebble *The Highland Clearances* (1963), London: Penguin Books 1969 p.277
22. David Craig *On the Crofter's Trail: in search of the Clearance Highlanders*, London: Jonathan Cape 1990 p.27.
23. *ibid* p.264.
24. *ibid* p.281.
25. *ibid* p.216.
26. *ibid* p.239.
27. *Northern Ensign* 25 Aug 1859, cited in Eric Richards: *The Highland Clearances: people, landlords and rural turmoil*, Edinburgh: Birlinn 2000 p.286.
28. J.W. Tonkin *Herefordshire*, London: B.T. Batsford 1977 p.30.

Chapter 3
Beating the bounds

*"In order to sense the atmosphere of the pre-indus-
trial rural scene it is desirable to leave the beaten
track (as far as this is still possible) and seek out
those corners of England and Wales where odd vestiges of that vanished era can be glimpsed. Such
places are usually quiet and sheltered, devoid of features likely to attract the attention of the compilers of
guidebooks... The traveller may come across them
quite unexpectedly, struck by an indefinable change
in the scale and quality of the landscape. One category comprises squatter settlements... The chaotic
morphology, with altered and patched-up cottages
(originally made of turf and branches) linked by narrow lanes twisting between the irregular enclosures
of the smallholdings, clearly reflects their haphazard
origins. Patterns of life such as these, based upon
rural economies, have shown themselves in some
cases to be remarkably resistant to change... Their
very locations — on the edge of heaths, moors or
forests, beyond the limits of manorial control or the
areas affected by enclosure — have aided their survival... Even in instances where, although the cottages are still inhabited, occupations have changed,
the remnants of the old economies refuse to pass
away, as the landscapes themselves demonstrate"*

Paul Coones & John Patten *The Penguin Guide to
the Landscape of England and Wales*[1]

This delicious description evokes a particular kind of village which, thanks to the dispersal of control over land
use, has developed in its own way. It reminds us of Richard
Mabey's account of Gilbert White's parish of Selborne, a

"kind of dense, luxuriant, muddled landscape" where "the lanes were more than just a system of by-ways" but "were landmarks, physical records of the past history and everyday experience of the parish." He goes on to describe how

> "Selborne flourished without the yolk of a squire. No single landowner determined the pattern of farming locally, or was able to institute widespread changes in the landscape. Instead there were a large number of owner-occupiers, copyholders and customary tenants, mostly with holdings of between ten and twenty acres... Selborne, consequently, was an independent even if not particularly prosperous community, and... a place where people could move about where they wished and exercise rights over a considerable area of common land."[2]

These were <u>open</u> as opposed to <u>close</u> parishes. This terminology dates from the early nineteenth century, with customary meanings that have since changed. The 'close' parish was originally one whose vestry meeting or parish council was, as Brian Short explains, "closed to all except a relative handful of its inhabitants. The meeting controlled the setting of a poor rate and how that rate should be spent, and it was therefore a very important aspect of country life. By contrast the 'open' parish functioned with a vestry meeting open to all ratepayers wishing to attend."[3] More recently the term has shifted its emphasis to the concentration or dispersal of land ownership. Dennis Mills has shown how concentration of land ownership implies a whole series of causal links where the squire is both magistrate and patron of the parish church, and provider of social facilities. There is likely to be early enclosure, with large farms, the control of game, and the absence of trades, crafts and industry, a small population and control of cottage accommodation and low poor rates with insufficient local labour supply. Politics would be conservative, and the squire might be a Peer or MP. There

28

would be a small number of nonconformists and an absence of manufacturing industry.

These, with endless local variations would characterise the 'close' parish, which would be likely to augment its supply of labour and services from any 'open' parish in the same area. In the ideal type for the 'open' parish, there would be a dispersal of landownership, with small farms, plenty of farm labourers being part-time farmers or tradesmen on their own account, for there would be a "well-developed range of trades and crafts". The lack of control over settlement would mean that there was plenty of cottage accommodation, a large population and high poor rates. Associated with these characteristics would be the emergence of radicalism in politics, of self-governing village organisations and of religious non-conformity. 'Open' parishes tended to be the birthplaces of industry.[4] They were also the places where an English peasantry survived.

The historian Mike Reed asked the question "Had the peasantry disappeared in 19th century England?" He cites the statement of Eric Hobsbawn that "England was a country of mainly large landlords, cultivated by tenant farmers, working the land with hired labourers"[5] and then modifies this stereotype, pointing out that "Since the census only asked those persons returning themselves as 'farmers' to give details of land held, it gives virtually no information about landholding by people in other occupations."[6] There were, in other words, an incalculable number of people who scraped a living in several, seasonal occupations, including cultivating their own patch.

There is, of course, another way of seeing the same phenomena. For B.A. Holderness, "An 'open' parish was overcrowded, insanitary, and ill regulated, with numerous small proprietors who let tumbledown cottages at exorbitant rents", while in 'close' parishes, he explains, "labourers employed by farmers in the parish, were compelled to walk to and from work. James Caird, in 1850, believed it very common to find agricultural labourers 'lodged at such a distance from their regular place of employment that they have to walk an hour out in the morning and an hour home in the evening, or from forty to fifty miles a week'"[7]

Centuries earlier, in Tudor times, a wave of enclosures by land-owners who sought to profit from the high price of wool had deprived commoners of their livelihood and obliged them to seek work elsewhere or become vagrants or squatters on the wastes on the edges of villages. R.J. Brown records that

> "Small encroachments of the wastes had been going on continually throughout the country with or without the authority of the manorial courts. Each one of these encroachments was made by someone in need of some kind of dwelling, who had no land on which to put it. So numerous were these encroachments that it became necessary by 1549 to pass an Act to regularise their position and make the land attached to these houses — as long as they did not exceed about two acres and 'doth no hurt' — free from any retribution by the owner of the waste"[8]

This was one minor recognition of the weakening of feudal power, which had been undermined by two centuries of peasant revolts between 1350 and 1550. Feudal ideology, as elsewhere in Europe, held that God had ordained that the monarch owned all land, and that his henchmen were privileged to hold their estates, administering the law and levying taxes, in return for raising armies to serve the king. These rights were passed down to the lords of the manor at a local level, whose serfs or villeins were tied to their lord's manor and served him in return for the right to cultivate a patch of land. The Court Baron and Court Leet were local courts, presided over by the lord or his steward. These are the bodies whose Court Rolls are the record of the building of squatter cottages, their destruction or survival. The story that usually unfolds to the researcher is that a fine is imposed, but that over the years

30

this is converted to a rent, and sometimes to the sale of the site. Christopher Hill explains that

> "England and Scotland were unique in Europe (except for Scandinavia) in having escaped from villeinage by the end of the sixteenth century, though some labour services survived — e.g. an act of 1555 imposed *corvée* duties on the roads on all able-bodied men for four days a year (the rich of course could buy themselves off)... This situation was not an unmixed blessing for the poorer peasants 'villeinage ends, the poor law begins', was Professor Tawney's terse comment... A statute of 1550 protected small cottagers building on wastes and commons. 47 years later it was laid down that no new cottages should be built without four acres of land attached; but J.P.s — themselves employers of wage labour — were in a position to enforce this or not as they pleased. A Judicial decision of 1605 laid it down that inhabitants as such had no common rights on the waste."[9]

For centuries the lives of the poor majority in rural England were dominated by the Poor Law and its ramifications, like the Settlement Act of 1697 which debarred strangers from entering a parish unless they had a Settlement Certificate in which their home parish agreed to take them back if they became in need of poor relief. Like the Workhouse, it was a hated institution that lasted into the 20th century. The attitude of manorial courts towards squatter houses depended on such factors as the current demand for labour. This determined how local manorial lords observed the Act of 1589 "against the erecting and maintaining of cottages" with the aim of "avoiding of the great inconveniences which are found to grow by the creating... of great numbers and multitudes of cottages." The Act was really directed against the poor, though as Dorothy George explained, it "allowed cottages for the impotent poor to be built on the village waste, with the consent of the lord of the manor and the parish officers. Other cottages might be licensed by the Justices in Quarter Sessions, and much of the business of the Sessions in the 17th century was taken up by the pressing question of cottages, with ordering their demolition or sanctioning their erection, always as a measure connected with poor relief and the parish poor."[10]

In 1662, after the restoration of the monarchy, the Act of Settlement restricted the movement of those villagers who were not freeholders or who could not afford a rent of £10 a year. It declared that "By some defect of the law, poor people are not restrained from going from one parish into another and, therefore do endeavour to settle themselves in those parishes where there is the best stock, the largest commons or wastes to build cottages, and the most woods for them to burn and destroy; and when they have consumed it, then to another parish and at last become rogues and vagabonds..."[11]

Between these two pieces of legislation directed against 'cottagers and paupers' — in other words against squatters — there occurred the most famous of what we would now call 'ideologically-inspired squats', that of Gerrard Winstanley and the Diggers at Walton-on-Thames in Surrey in 1649. Setting the background, Christopher Hill records that

"The Midlands rising of 1607, in which we first come across the names Levellers and Diggers, was caused by enclosure. Risings in western England in the late twenties and early thirties turned in large part on royal enclosure and rights of squatters in the forests. Oliver Cromwell first won a national reputation as the defender of commoners who opposed the draining of the Fens. Just as the breakdown of the authority of the state church in the sixteen-forties allowed underground sects to surface, so the breakdown of secular authority

32

released a series of riots against enclosure all over the country."[12]

It was in his pamphlet *The New Law of Righteousness*, written in January 1669, that Winstanley set out his criticism of the private appropriation of land:

"And this is the beginning of particular interest, buying and selling the Earth, from one particular hand to another, saying 'This is mine,' upholding this particular propriety by a law of government of his own making, and thereby restraining other fellow-creatures from seeking nourishment from their Mother Earth. So that though a man was bred up in a Land, yet he must not work it for himself where he would, but for him who had bought part of the Land or had came to it by inheritance of his deceased parents, and called it his own Land. So that he who had no Land was to work for small wages for those who called the Land theirs. Thereby some are lifted up in the chair of tyranny, and others trod under the footstool of misery, as if the Earth were made for a few, and not for all men."[13]

All through his pamphlets and public manifestos of those years, Winstanley returns to this theme, declaring for example in his *New Year's Gift for the Parliament and Army*, "Therefore I say, the Common Land is my own Land, equal with my fellow Commoners; and our true propriety by the Law of Creation. It is every ones, but not one single ones..."

The Diggers' invasion of the land next to Campe Close at St George's Hill at Walton-on-Thames in Surrey began on Sunday 1st April 1649, and the Council of State was immediately informed by Henry Sanders, a local resident, that these people were sowing the ground with parsnips, carrots and beans, with the intention of restoring "the ancient community of enjoying the fruits of the earth."

The Council of State sent the letter on the same day to Lord Fairfax, Lord General of the Armed Forces of the Commonwealth, urging him to send some force of horse "to Cobham in Surrey and thereabouts, with orders to disperse the people so met, and to prevent the like for the future, that a malignant and disaffected party may not under colour of such ridiculous people have any opportunity to rendezvous themselves in order to do a greater mischief."[15]

The Diggers were harried and eventually transferred themselves to Cobham Heath, a mile or two away, where after further persecution, and the burning of their huts and furniture, their settlement was abandoned, exactly eight years after the original squat. According to Christopher Hill, "by the beginning of 1650 other Digger colonies were beginning to appear, at Wellingborough in Northamptonshire, Cox Hall in Kent, Iver in Buckinghamshire, Barnet in Hertfordshire, Enfield in Middlesex, Dunstable in Bedfordshire, Bosworth in Leicestershire and at unknown places in Gloucestershire and Nottinghamshire."[16] But by the end of that year the movement had collapsed everywhere.

This did not mean that squatting had collapsed. Winstanley and his fellow Diggers chose to make a public demonstration of the activity usually done by stealth. However, the 1662 Act of Settlement sought to ensure that the poor stayed in the parishes of their birth. Robert Humphreys, the historian of the travelling poor, notes that this Act can be seen as "a camouflaged reintroduction of the principle of villeinage — an extreme form of parish isolationism."[17] And he mentions as one of the consequences, the attraction of outlaw communities whose residents would really have wished to be incorporated into settled life:

"Especially attractive to poor travellers were villages which still retained extensive commons in fen, moorland or forest. Newcomers could squat while scratching around to support themselves off the land. Christopher Hill has described how beneath the surface calm of rural England there was a 'seething fluidity' of forest squatters. They included itinerant craftsmen and building labourers, unemployed men and women seeking work, strolling players, minstrels and jugglers, pedlars and quack doctors, gypsies, vagabonds and tramps. For these people, odds and ends of casual or seasonal work were their best hope. They made footholds wherever newly squatted areas escaped the machinery of the parish. Some travellers used old squats near to where labour had been in demand in the hope that opportunity would again arise."[18]

A ritual that maintained the closeness of the close parish and which was hard to enact in those wide-open parishes surrounded by unsettled wastes, was the ancient ceremony of the Perambulation or Beating the Bounds, which has its origins in the Roman festivals of *Terminalia* and *Ambarvalis*. The oral historian George Ewart Evans explained that the two pagan ceremonies were Christianised, and joined in the ritual called Beating the Bounds, celebrated at Rogationtide, on the fifth Sunday after Easter.

"The Rogationtide procession was a means both of re-affirming the parish boundaries and of entreating God to send good weather and fair fortune to the growing crops. At the head of the procession was a priest; following was a crowd of people, some carrying wands or sticks. The priest stopped at various well-known landmarks — usually an ancient tree – and read the gospel for the day, sanctifying the occasion and at the same time conferring the incidental title of Gospel Oak on the tree which in many villages, for instance the Suffolk villages of Polstead, has long outlasted the ceremony."[19]

Denis Pym, a resident of the village mentioned by George Ewart Evans, told me that there is a cut off point at a certain age. "Above it, people know every field, footpath, edge, boundary and copse in the parish. Below it, they have very attenuated mental maps." The same thing is found in towns. City teachers, even the most experienced, are so accustomed to mobility, access to transport and social competence in getting around that they are continually surprised to find that so many of the children they teach lead lives confined to a few streets. I knew a south London teacher who invented an instant tradition of local environmental walks to remedy this deficiency and called it Beating the Bounds of the Catchment Area.

She was building on a ritual of immemorial antiquity, which in the days before universal access to maps was a means of passing on parish wisdom and of hearing the priest say: "Cursed is he that transgresseth the bounds of his neighbour." Evans explained that "The bearer of the sticks, and the young boys in the procession also had an essential part in the ceremony: at certain points of the boundary — usually those susceptible of dispute — the men proceeded to beat the landmark with their sticks, then as an 18th-century record had it: 'whipping ye boys by way of remembrance and stopping their cry with some halfpence.'"[20]

The Open Spaces Society, founded in 1865 as the Commons, Open Spaces and Footpaths Preservation Society, has for more than half a century been encouraging the continuance by parish and community councils and local groups of the ancient practice of Beating the Bounds on Rogation Sunday. It urges that the children should be taken along, but bumped gently. The Society is involved in continual local efforts to preserve public access to open space and to secure more of it.[21] The existence of the tradition of beating the bounds is a reminder that squatters could be in conflict not only with Lords of the Manor, but with other commoners, and that both might be in conflict with enclosing landlords.

Different historians give varying emphases to the parochial perambulations in Rogation week. For Maurice Keen the custom was "in order to warn neighbouring communities against encroachment."[22] For Bob Bushaway, "these manor processions had little spiritual significance, and were intended as an administrative device to regulate use of the lord's estate by his tenants and to prevent encroachments or other abuses by squatters, or by other tenants seeking to enhance their holdings or rights."[23] But for George Ewart Evans the exact determination of the parish boundaries was, for hundreds of years, the overriding reason: the establishment of the parish as the unit of poor-law administration, making it in effect "a kind of closed compound." For,

"By making it chargeable for its own poor, legislation brought it about that the parish officers — the churchwardens, the constable and the overseers of the poor — felt it one of their main functions to see that they had as few poor as possible in the village. And in the event, this meant not so much an attention to the over-all economy of the parish as a determination to get rid of the poor they had by transporting them elsewhere, and by preventing any pauper or likely pauper from outside their boundaries from setting foot within. Before being eligible for poor relief a person had to *gain a settlement* in a parish, and in many cases this was as difficult as the entry of the proverbial rich man into heaven."[24]

Evans stressed that the hounding of the poor from one parish to another was enormously expensive, the suffering was tremendous, and that the procedure "made a mockery of the word charity from which it has never recovered." He spent years recording the memories of the last rural generation to suffer the indignities and humiliations of the Poor Law, and knew the bitterness of people's family memories.

References

1. Paul Coones and John Patten *The Penguin Guide to the Landscape of England and Wales*, Harmondsworth: Penguin Books 1986 p.230.
2. Richard Mabey *Gilbert White: A biography of the author of The Natural History of Selborne*, London: Century 1986 p.29.
3. Brian Short "The evolution of contrasting communities within rural England" in Brian Short (ed) *The English Rural Community: image and reality*, Cambridge University Press 1992 pp. 28-29.
4 Dennis Mills and Brian Short "Social change and social conflict in nineteenth-century England: the use of the open-close village model" *Journal of Peasant Studies* Vol 10 No 4, 1983.
5. Eric Hobsbawm *Industry and Empire*, Harmondsworth: Penguin Books 1969 p.98.
6. Mick Reed "The Peasantry of Nineteenth-Century Rural England: A Neglected Class?" *History Workshop* Vol 1B 1984.
7. B.A. Holderness "'Open' and 'Close' Parishes in England in the Eighteenth and Nineteenth Centuries" *Agricultural History Review* Vol 20 1972 pp. 126-139.
8. R.J. Brown *The English Country*, London: Robert Hale 1979 p.28.
9. Christopher Hill *Reformation to Industrial Revolution 1530-1780*, Harmondsworth: Penguin Books 1969 p. 6.
10. M. Dorothy George *England in Transition* (1931), Harmondsworth: Penguin Books 1953.
11. 14 Charles II C.12 (1662) *Act of Settlement and Removal*.
12. Christopher Hill (ed) *Gerrard Winstanley: the law of freedom and other writings*, Harmondsworth: Penguin Books 1973 p.21.
13. Gerrard Winstanley *The New Law of Righteousness* (1649) in G.H. Sabine (ed) *Works of Gerrard Winstanley*, Ithica: Cornell University Press 1941.
14. Gerrard Winstanley *A New-year's Gift for the Parliament and Army* in Hill *op cit* p.184.
15. Lewis H. Berens *The Digger Movement in the Days of the Commonwealth* (1906), London: Holland Press and Merlin Press 1961 p.37.
16. Christopher Hill *op cit* p.30.
17. Robert Humphreys *No Fixed Abode: a history of responses to the roofless and the rootless in Britain*, London: Macmillan 1999 p.67.

18. *ibid* p.64.
19 George Ewart Evans *The Pattern Under the Plough*, London: Faber & Faber 1966 p.104-5.
20. *ibid*
21. Open Spaces Society, 25a Bell Street, Henley-on-Thames, Oxon RG9 2BA.
22. Maurice Keen *English Society in the Later Middle Ages 1348-1500*, London: Allen Lane, the Penguin Press 1990 p.49.
23. Bob Bushaway: *By Rite*, London: Junction Books 1982 p.68.
24. George Ewart Evans *op cit* p.106.

Stone house, Greenway Bank, Baddeley Edge, Staffordshire. The original coal-miner's cottage on the left was later doubled in size. (PHOTO: 1993, IAN BAILEY).

Chapter 4
Ty unnos: the one-night house in Wales

"But probably in no area of activity was the poorer country-people's native ingenuity tested more fully, than in building the dwellings that they very frequently had to erect for themselves, home-made homes indeed. These largely landless houses are known as cottages and their inhabitants as cottagers. Cottagers had to build their own homes, either personally or communally, for they could not afford to hire building contractors. Because of the nature of these buildings — they used poor-quality materials and did not last long — we know little about them until the middle of the eighteenth century, although their virtual absence shows that they were not good enough to last for more than a century or two, in contrast to farmhouses which survived fairly commonly from the seventeenth century..."

Eurwyn Wiliam *Home-made Homes: Dwellings of the rural poor in Wales[1]*

The idea of the one-night house is woven into Welsh history, where it is seen as relating to the imposition of Norman land law. The country has a mountainous heartland, rainy and windswept, surrounded by a fertile lowland fringe. Rainfall has carved deep valleys edging up the hillsides. Wales has had a pastoral economy since the Iron Age, and a seasonal migration of both humans and animals to the uplands. The historical geographer E.G. Bowen sums up the Welsh hillside experience:

"The summer dwelling was frequently referred to as the Hafod (*haf* = summer). This basic economy was,

41

however, slowly undermined by the Normans and the Plantagenetes who introduced feudal conceptions of tenure and service — a process which culminated in the decrees of Henry VIII. These, and many other changes, involved the enclosure of the lower fringes of the moorland, while the great Enclosure Acts of the 18th and 19th centuries led to the appropriation of vast unenclosed pasture areas. In this way many of the original *hafodai* (summer dwellings) were turned into self-contained farms. Meanwhile, wholesale squatting on the waste occurred, especially in those areas where the landlords were less vigilant."[2]

Professor Bowen's account goes on to describe how this popular defiance of legal tenure reversed the direction of the seasonal movement of sheep. As the former *hafod* became a permanent farm, sheep would be moved down to winter on other farms and the uplands became the place where sheep and cattle were reared rather than fattened for the market.

This pressure on mountain land, wastes and commons came from big landlords and farmers anxious to extend their property as well as from the landless poor in a period of rising population. In his study of the background to the Rebecca Riots of 1843-44 in South Wales (which sought redress for discrimination against the poor in increased toll and tithes) David Jones explains how

"Much of this encroachment, which amounted to thousands of acres, was carried out without permission from the various manorial courts, but it did conform to familiar patterns. Sometimes, as in the case of widow Mary Rees of Llandybie, a community helped to establish a new home for one of its members, and families adjoining uncultivated mountain land did likewise for their relatives. Yet, increasingly, new freeholds were being created 'secretly' by enterprising individuals, some unknown to their neighbours. 'Within the last 10 years a great number of cottages have been erected upon the mountain wastes and sheepwalks...', ran a common complaint by Cardiganshire landowners at the turn of the century, 'some of whom are parishioners having settlements there and others are strangers, and they usually enclose about 6 acres of land with each cottage, under an idea that cottages erected on the waste with each a portion of land annexed to them cannot be pulled down.'"[3]

David Jones provides fascinating detail of the struggle for land in those years, even though he is at pains to stress that "despite claims that the Rebeccites were levellers, challenging property rights, the ownership of land was not a major issue." He explains that

"The 'strangers' were the squatters of Welsh myth and history, 'the scum of this and other counties'. They settled on land, under the old custom of *ty unnos*, whereby a person was entitled to the freehold of whatever shelter he or she could build in a night and of the land within a stone's throw. Such encampments were not universally popular, for they cut across the rights of local farmers, interfered with the traditional sheep walks, and there were fears that the poorest squatters might become a burden on the rates. Their homesteads became a source of 'ever-lasting quarrels', and of innumerable court cases. In the latter there was an assumption that if squatters were allowed to remain on the land for more than one generation they had established a legal right to it; after that they could, as one prosecutor put it, 'snap their fingers at everyone and become a Cardiganshire squire'."[4]

Of course, the people who really could snap their fingers at everyone *were* the lords of the manor. Jones cites the case of Mrs Lewis, a widow on Clydau common whose house was pulled down in 1838, even though it had stood for 20 years, and, "Significantly, the man behind this destruction was Pryse Pryse, MP and lord of the manor." And he describes how the same triumphant landlord was able, through enclosure to take away subsidiary rights:

"In Cardiganshire parliamentary enclosure undermined a variety of fishing practices and gleaning customs, not least the cutting of turf, peat, clay and wood. In the 1820s, when people finally appreciated how closely these rights had been circumscribed, there were ugly incidents, with fences pulled down, property set on fire, and animals maimed. Amongst the loudest protesters were female fuel sellers and rush-collecting hatters. The latter declared their determination to ignore all restrictive legislation, but Pryse Pryse, who had bought part of the great Gorsfochno bog in an enclosure award, proved a worthy opponent and the most militant hatters were imprisoned in 1843 for six months."[5]

Describing the consequences of enclosure in South-West Wales, David Jones stresses that it was always more of an exercise in power and finance than an experiment in improved agriculture, and that

"Since the mid-eighteenth century those landowners most aware of the latest commercial and legal developments had begun a prolonged attempt to secure and establish all their extensive rights of property. The Crown, which owned large tracts of Cardiganshire, and lesser amounts of land in the other two counties, passed slowly to the front of this campaign. By the 1830s its officers were enforcing payment of Crown rent and dues, and its

44

courts repeatedly condemned encroachments by freeholders and squatters..."[6]

By the next decade, long-established householders and self-builders were being evicted and the Rural Police were being used as the Landlord's agents:

"A number of squatters were legally and physically removed from their holdings as a result of enclosure, or they left their homes rather than pay the purchase price and the increased costs of continued occupation. David Gower, a carpenter of Pembrey, who built a cottage on Craig Chapel common in 1810, discovered almost twenty years later that enclosure commissioners disputed his property rights and sold his house and market gardens for £50. Thirteen years later he was 84 years of age, and, so it was claimed, totally dependent on others for help, bare-footed, hungry, and unable to persuade the Poor Law Guardians to increase his relief of 2s.6d. per week. Others, like Edward Evans of Gwnnws parish in Cardiganshire, managed to survive the trauma of an enclosure award only to find years later that bright new agents and professional policemen were determined to enact the squatter's nightmare."[7]

This implacable determination to eliminate squatters contrasts sharply with popular belief in the inviolable nature of the tradition. Instances from mid-Glamorgan include the rule for the appropriate size of the patch of land around the house to be enclosed. In his 1940 study of *The Welsh Home*, Iorwerth Peate, later Keeper of the Welsh Folk Museum, explained how, according to his old informants, squatters set up their homes on common wastelands:

"Such 'squatting' seems to have been common from the seventeenth to the nineteenth century... The method generally adopted was to erect a *ty un nos*, a house built in one night, and enclose around it a small area of ground... These houses were sometimes round, but often rectangular. The intending proprietor and his friends proceeded... at nightfall, and with great activity, to cut clods... of the green sward. When a quantity of the turf had been cut... part of the company commenced building up the walls with the clods having been raised sufficiently high, the previously prepared roof was put on and thatched with all speed, so that the roof should be completed and smoke ascend through the chimney ere the sun rose. All this having been done the active builder could... bid defiance to all... rights... of the owner of the soil. The quantity of land that the proprietor... could... claim... was decided by his throwing an axe from the door... in various directions, the hedge being planted along this line."[8]

While Dr Peate was writing his book, the quarterly *Revue de Folklore Français* (the last issue to reach Britain for six years) included a paper on "*Les maisons construites en une nuit*",[9] which was read with especial interest by another Welsh amateur of local history, R.U. Sayce. He had first heard of the Welsh version of this belief as a boy living near Welshpool in Montgomeryshire. He gathered together his accumulated knowledge in a brief note in *Folk-Lore*, the transactions of the Folk-Lore Society in 1942,[10] and in a longer article in the Montgomeryshire Collections in the same year,[11] hoping that in more settled times it would be possible to trace the international distribution of the one-night house. He explained that,

"Many people in Montgomeryshire must be familiar with the belief that if a man built a cottage on a piece of wasteland, *in one night*, he thereby acquired a freehold right to it; but opinions probably differ as to whether this is merely an unfounded belief or a survival of some ancient popular custom. I have collected a few notes on the subject and am publishing them in order to start a hare which I hope competent historians will hunt down. Although the custom was well-known in the last century, there are now many middle-aged people who have never heard of it."

Mr Sayce was writing over half a century ago, and the competent history he was hoping for seems never to have been written, since over the decades contributors of further observations to the pages of the journal now called *Folklore* invariably refer back to his article. He built his account around the information gathered in Gilbert Slater's famous history, from 1907, of the effect of the enclosures of the common fields:

"The parish of ...., in the county of Montgomeryshire, is about five miles long by two miles broad. It consists for the most part of a hill, lying between a river and one of its contributaries. The hill rises to about 900 feet above sea level, and contains no unenclosed land... On this hill most of the cottage holdings are to be found, usually in some sheltered hollow near a spring or a running stream... Previous to the Enclosure Act, passed early in the nineteenth century, the greater part of the hill was open... The unenclosed portion of the hill was used as a common pasture by all the farmers whose land adjoined it, and the amount of stock each one was allowed to feed on it was roughly regulated by the size of his holding."

"About 120 years ago a number of the poorest peasantry began settling on the common land. There was a general understanding that if a house was raised during the night so that the builders were able to cause smoke to issue from the chimney by sunraise, they thereby established a right of possession which none could gainsay. Timber in the neighbouring wood was abundant and cheap, so an intended squatter had little difficulty in procuring the material for his cottage. With the help of a few friends he procured sufficient wood for the framework, and then selected a convenient site in a sheltered spot with a southern aspect, and marked down the foundations of his future dwelling. When all the preparations were made, he gathered together all the help he could, and in the dusk of the evening had all his materials conveyed to the selected spot.

Rough stonework was laid to form the foundations and chimney end of the cottage, and then the framework was quickly set up. The panels were interwoven with stout laths, and covered with clay, over which was smeared a coating of lime-plaster, while a roof of thatch completed the edifice. Windows were not, for a time, considered necessary, but the entrance was carefully secured by a stout door. Then just as the dawn was breaking, a fire was kindled in the hearth, and the curl of smoke above the rude chimney told the workers that they could relax their efforts..."[12]

This is the classic account of the one-night house: others had a few additonal features, but for completeness, Sayce cited two more. One, a study of ancient land tenure, reported that "no reference to this custom is to be found in the Welsh 'Laws' or Surveys; and it probably arose from the negligence of the crown officials during that last two or three centuries." It also linked the custom to marriage, since it "presumed the right of any newly married resident to the cottage which he had himself, with the help of his friends, built upon the wasteland of the township..."[13]

Another account introduced the terms Clod Hall and *caban-un-nos*, for the cabin built in a night. It reported (in 1875) that the last house built in the parish of Llansantffraid, some thirty years earlier,

> "had quickly to succumb to modern law and justice for the rightful owner of the soil in spite of the curling smoke, thatched roof, and completed house, sent old Sally Morris and her friends to other wastes to try their better luck at erecting a *caban-un-nos*."[14]

One of his informants, Professor E.A. Lewis told him that in Radnorshire the common name for this kind of overnight house was 'Labour in Vain', which suggests, he explained, that many never succeeded in establishing their right to freehold. "Some squatters, however, were allowed to continue in occupation of their cottages on agreeing to pay a rent, often only a nominal one, to the lord of the manor." Seeking answers to his questions on the legal standing of squatters' cottages and holdings, Mr Sayce studied a government document from 1844, the *Report of the Select Committee on Commons Inclosures*.[15]

This confirmed for him that rights of common attached to certain lands or houses included the right to turn on to the waste in summer as many cattle as the farm could support in the winter.

> "The waste might belong to the Crown, or be under the jurisdiction of the lord of the manor. If it was of wide extent a few small encroachments might be of little importance, but a considerable number of enclosures on a small waste would seriously restrict the summer grazing of the local

farmers who had right of common. The lord of the manor held his court once or twice a year, according to the custom. At the court the homage was sworn. It consisted usually of the freeholders and principal tenants. The lord of the manor could give permission for a cottage to be built on the waste, but in most manors, though not all, he had to have the assent of a jury consisting of local farmers."[16]

But "many encroachers apparently did not trouble to obtain assent of the manor court, and violated the right of common which had belonged to local farmers since time out of mind." However, in parts of Radnorshire, "the farmers having right of common, periodically turned out in a body, destroyed the tenements, and threw open the enclosures; but the encroachers soon re-established the fences."[17]

The impression Mr Sayce derived from the Select Committee evidence was that the poorest peasants began settling on common land from about 1790 and that "the movement seems to have gone on until somewhere about 1844." In other words, it coincided with the greatest activity in Parliamentary Enclosures. The Committee was told by the Rt. Hon. T.F. Lewis that squatting had become very general in Radnorshire. After the road was constructed from Lampeter to Llandovery, very many encroachments on the commons were made. "Similar evidence was given by Colonel Wood for the Great Forest of Brecknock." In his evidence to the Committee, Mr R. Banks, a solicitor who lived at Kington in Herefordshire, said that in his opinion, enclosure of common land

"would prevent a vast number of encroachments which are daily taking place, which are increasing in various districts which are well known. I could name a place in Brecknockshire, called Mutton Street, where there are a great many squatters; it is a perfect den of sheep-stealers. I could name another place in the parish of Beguildy, nearly on the borders of Montgomeryshire, a place called the Scrubs; it is within the Crown manor of Ugre, where there is a similar colony, and several of parties were tried at the last quarter sessions of the county, for stealing and driving the flocks of sheep off the common into a wood, getting the wool off their backs in any way that they could effect it, and slaughtering the sheep to prevent detection..."[18]

As though conscious of a certain prejudice in these comments, Mr Sayce commented that "It is probable that conditions varied a good deal from place to place, and that the success of an encroachment depended on the site, the quality of the land, relations with neighbours, and, of course, on the personal character of the encloser."[19]

The opinions heard by the Select Committee in 1844 were also examined by Dr James Moir in his study of squatters in Herefordshire just over the English border, described in Chapter 8 below. He notes that while virtually every moral failing was attributed to the squatters on the commons, when he examined detailed police records from the period, the first striking feature he found was the low level and general pettiness of the crimes reported.

References
1. Eurwyn Wiliam *Home-made Homes: dwellings of the rural poor in Wales*, Cardiff: National Museum of Wales 1988 p.10.
2. E.G. Bowen *Wales: A Physical, Historical and Regional Geography*, London: Methuen and Co 1957 p.272.
3. David J.V. Jones *Rebecca's Children: a study of rural society, crime and protest*, Oxford: Clarendon Press 1989 pp. 52-3.
4. *ibid* p.53.
5. *ibid* p.55.
6. *ibid* p.53.
7. *ibid* p.55.

8.   Iorwerth C. Peate *The Welsh House*, London: Honourable Society of Cymmrodorion 1940, Liverpool: Brython Press 1946.

9.   G. Jeanton "Les maisons construites en une nuit" *Revue de Folklore Français* April-June 1939.

10. R.U. Sayce "The One-Night House, and its Distribution" *Folk-Lore* June 1942, Vol LIII pp. 161-163.

11. R.U. Sayce "Popular Enclosures and the One-Night House" *Montgomeryshire Collections*, Vol XIVII, Part 2, 1942 pp. 109-120.

12. Gilbert Slater *The English Peasantry and the Enclosure of the Common Fields*, London: 1907.

13. Palmer and Owen *A History of Ancient Tenures in North Wales and the Welsh Marches*, London: 1910.

14. *Byegones relating to Wales and the Border Counties*, May 19th 1875, cited by Sayce *op cit*.

15. *Report of the Select Committee on Commons Enclosure, together with Minutes of Evidence*, London: 1844.

16. Sayce *op cit* p.112.

17. *ibid* p.114.

18. *ibid* p.114.

19. *ibid* p.114.

Chapter 5
Mushroom Town:
a continuing Welsh tradition

"When you have built your house, it does not belong to you. Part of it will belong to me, and that part will grow year by year. I will have a few stones this year, and the stones will grow year by year, and I will take your house piece by piece. When you are an old man half of it will belong to me, and when you are dead it will pass to my son, and not to yours."

David Lloyd George: *Better Times*

Lloyd George was assuming the landlord's voice in order to attack the concept of leasehold, when the house built by its occupier reverted to the legal owner of otherwise worthless land on which a ground-rent had been paid for the whole period of the lease. These fears weighed even more heavily on the occupiers of land with no form of tenure other than the customary 'squatters' rights'. This is one reason why the misgivings of the amateur historian R.U. Sayce that future generations would forget the custom of the one-night house have not been fulfilled. Its existence has become one of those items of local lore that people pass on to their grandchildren. There is a Gaelic phrase *fas na h-aon oidhche*, meaning "a one-night's growth" which describes the equivalent in Ireland. It is also used to describe a mushroom, and *Mushroom Town* is the name of a novel by Oliver Onions, published in 1914, the plot of which revolves around the building of a *Hafod Unnos* — a one-night summer dwelling in a resort on the North Wales coast by four brothers from Lancashire.[2]

Writing in 1944, Mr M.W. Gill drew attention to the existence of "Hafod-unnos near Llangerniew, Denbighshire, a small village which is now known by the name of its first house," adding that "As a South Wales example, many years ago I was told by Mr George Eyre Evans that certain hovels then standing under the shadow of Carmarthen Gaol were the result of unauthorised 'squatting on a kind of no-man's land."[3]

Similarly, John Williams, whose native parish is Llanddeiniolen, Gwynedd, in the old county of Caernarfon, learned from his grandfather of the battle between the Assheton Smith family and the builders of one-night houses or "morning surprises." His grandfather told him too, of *Yr Ynys Lwyd*, the instant home from the turn of the 20th century of Robert and Mari Lewis. He explains how the parish was divided between the valley floor and the high ground, formerly common land, on the mountain slopes:

> "Early in the nineteenth century, the squirearchy – already with investments in the slate industry, land-hungry and needing easier access to the quarries to gain rights of way for transport — eventually took possession of this land by a mixture of open force and subterfuge, pushing their boundaries higher towards the ranges. Their cause against that of the illiterate populace was facilitated by the enclosure acts, and it is estimated that more than 3,000 acres were enclosed in Llanddeiniolen in the opening years of the last century."[4]

From local records, John Williams tells the story of a hopeful couple who in September 1809 built a *ty unnos* on common land in the manor of Dinorwig:

> "No sooner was the deed done, than representatives of Assheton Smith — a solicitor and a magistrate supported by constables — arrived at the site and ordered the occupants to leave. The squatters, however, barricaded the building and prepared to resist a forced entry. The besiegers then began to tear

down the walls, whereupon reinforcements for the occupants arrived from the quarry. There was a set-to during which the defenders seem to have made liberal use of stones, turf and boiling water. The officials had to withdraw with bruised heads and scalded backs, but they later returned to find an even larger crowd facing them. Eventually the Riot Act was read, contravention of which was a capital offense. The majority of the resisters dispersed, but a nucleus, including one Ellis Evans, remained after the given hour had expired. He and others later had to flee the district."[5]

His account is amplified by that of Eurwyn Wiliam, who reveals that the lawyer concerned, John Evans of Caernarfon, who served as a bailiff for Thomas Assheton Smith, had carefully listed the cottages erected on Llanddeiniolen common. Forty cottages had been erected between 1789 and 1808, twelve of them in 1795-96:

"Thomas Pierce had a house and a cowhouse, the former measuring 30 by 20 by 8 feet, and the latter 15 by 10 by 6½ feet (9.1 m by 6m by 2.4m, and 4.6m by 3m by 2m). They had been built ten years before the survey of 1809 and were still in good condition. Ellis Evans had a good building not quite finished, measuring 27 by 18 feet (8.2m by 5.5m). Lowri Jones's cottage, built only fourteen years before, on the other hand, was in very poor condition."[6]

Apparently Ellis Evans had assembled a team of stone-masons to help him build, but the masons were warned off by John Evans, so that

"In desperation, Ellis Evans gathered his friends together, and, in the words of the document, in a day and a night, the walls were raised, and green turves were thrown over the roof."[7]

The rich encroachers had won, but still felt the need to harry the poor encroachers. John Williams quotes a surviving self-congratulatory letter from Jon Evans to Lord Bulkeley:

"My Lord: I may now say as to the Llanddeiniolen Rioters that I fought and conquered. I went up yesterday with the Reverend Williams and eight constables and took three of the Rioters and conveyed them to the gaol. I expect to take two or three tomorrow. I have completely tamed the Tigers, they are truly sensible of their error... they have offered to give up all their encroachment — I have written to Mr A. Smith on the subject."[8]

Ellis Evans fled south to become a coal miner, following the pattern of population movement that was to become general in the 19th century. Eurwyn William explained that,

"Whereas the bulk of the population lived on or near the land at the beginning of the century, by its end, a large majority were concentrated into one corner of the country and depended on industrial work for their living. Younger sons of poor farms were glad to escape the monotony and drudgery of their life, but it was the landless cottagers who were most affected by this trend. After 1850, more and more fled the land and exchanged its hardships for a different but equally terrible life in the blossoming iron and coal mines and their service industries."[9]

As the social historian Roger Laidlaw put it, "South Wales exploded in the latter part of the nineteenth century and sucked millions into the newly created communities in the valleys and on the coastal strip."[10] His concern was with the older Flintshire coalfield in the North, harder to work and far less accessible to the export markets, and he examined the village of Rhosllanerchrugog, which, as technical advances made deeper pits possible, expanded from a population of 1,244 in 1811 into one of 3,467 by 1841:

"The population of the village originated from the upland farming communities that lay to the West. Their migration was prompted by the enclosure of common land which deprived many small farmers of their livelihoods and the agricultural depression after the Napoleonic wars... During the first stage of industrialisation, the mining communities sprang up among the pits which mined the outcrops on the moorland edge, and their inhabitants constructed their own houses, either by encroaching on common land as squatters or by paying a nominal rent to a ground landlord."[11]

Roger Laidlaw cites a lawsuit by Sir Watkin Williams Wynn in 1819 to challenge the right of tenure claimed by squatters on land for which Sir Watkin had leased the mineral royalties.[12] Everything to do with land, even the barren rocky moorlands, had become a commodity.

The number of cottagers employed as farm labourers had fallen to 34,000 in Wales by 1851 and to only 23,000 in 1871, but cottagers employed in industry very frequently had a small holding or *tyddyn* on the land around their cottage where the quarryman's or miner's wife kept pigs, cows and chickens. However, by 1876 the Inspector of Mines was reporting that the quarrymen "generally live in places where the luxury of a garden cannot be bought at any price."[13] In his study of the slate quarrying communities, R. Merfyn Jones found that,

"In Llanberis, the majority of houses seem to have been built by quarrymen themselves or bought by them from local builders, though ground rent continued to be paid to the two main landlords in the area... The ground rent charged and the implications of the leasehold system in general, cause considerable resentment amongst the quarrymen. D.G. Williams of Blaenau Ffestiniog, for example, who paid 15s. ground rent, felt in 1885 that he was being overcharged by 14s.6d., since 'before the house was built, the land would not keep a hen alive'. In 1892 the North Wales Quarrymen's Union attacked the Penrhyn quarry manager's evidence to the Royal Commission on Labour in the same vein. What, they asked, was 'the value of the boggy and rocky land on which the houses are built before these poor quarrymen put their labour, and their hard-earned money, and their life-blood in them?' And, moreover, it was added that the 'poor boggy mountain land... was common land in the recollection of some old inhabitants'.[14]

To the quarrymen, as well as the tenant farmers, there was an even greater injustice in the fact that when leases expired, the whole property reverted to the ground landlord.

Inevitably, when landlords were seen as extortionate, and when industrial workers lived in housing rented from their employers (and would lose the family's home if they lost their job) the one-night house was evoked in the popular memory as a reminder of the days when every man had a natural right to house his family and to keep a pig and a cow. Dennis Griffiths of the small brick-making town of Buckley in Flintshire, grew up with the traditional belief in the possibility of

"a poor wandering family pitching their tent on the common, building a hearth and boiling their pot thereon in the course of one summer's day and night, and claiming from ancient usage their right to the spot. Thus, a hut so built, was gradually made into a decent cottage: the surrounding ground, from a mere yard of scant dimensions, would become a yard and a garden, and patch after patch being cribbed and enclosed. In the course of a few years a little holding was created in the midst or on the margin of a common. These practices were often winked at by the Parish in favour of a poor, industrious, large family, who were thus provided for instead of becoming objects of parochial relief. If the intrusion remained undisturbed for sixty years, it became a freehold property."[15]

This, of course, was an evocation of the ideal, seldom encountered in real life. In his study of Rhosllanerchrugog, Roger Laidlaw cited a series of responses over time, from George Borrow in *Wild Wales* stumbling on a small settlement of "grimy looking huts" in 1854, to the report for 1936 of the local Medical Officer of Health that there were still at least 750 examples in the village of what was known as the "chamber house" consisting of "a one-storied building containing a general living room and leading from it a bedroom." Laidlaw noted how

"Nineteenth century observers were shocked at the appalling sanitary conditions which prevailed in the village and were virtually unanimous in describing the villagers as the architects of their own dwellings, as the authors of their own misfortunes. Henry Vaughan Johnson, a sub-commissioner for the 1847 Welsh Education Commission, condemned the dwellings and the degrading habits of the villagers who inhabited them. He beheld Rhos and declared that 'nothing could more forcibly illustrate the imperfect nature of indigenous civilisation if isolated and unaided.' A visitor to the area in 1899 found the inhabitants of Ponciau still wallowing in the two-roomed 'wigwams' favoured by their ancestors."[16]

But by 1919, a chance visitor, whose interest was not sanitation was already marvelling at the uniqueness of the home-made architecture of the poor. He was J.H. Jones, editor of a Welsh language periodical and he came to Rhos to adjudicate at a village *eisteddfod*:

> "The shapes of the houses and the streets of Rhos are strange, very strange. The village would surely look very peculiar if seen from an aeroplane! Most of the people have succeeded in building their houses where they please, having the shape they please and facing whichever direction they please. One house seems to be within spitting distance of the next and I am sure that there is not one figure in the whole of Geometry that could completely define Rhos. Rhos is the most visual living proof that the world has ever seen that man has a free will, because no laws and bye-laws imposed from outside authorities would ever have succeeded in building houses in this manner."[17]

The Welsh squatter houses are by now a matter of history. Every few years the local press reports that a local authority has served a demolition order on the elderly resident of an isolated cottage lacking water, electricity and drainage, where the occupant demands to be left in peace. In his history of Welsh rural workers' housing, Jeremy Lowe sums up the history of the *ty unnos*:

> "Such houses were bound to be poorly built and the lawful proprietors of the commons preferred that they should be so. They tolerated the squatters because it suited them to do so. In the nineteenth century, most of the commons were enclosed and many of the squatters lost such 'rights' as Welsh custom had given them. They became once more rent-paying tenants of the big landowners or they were evicted so that their homes could be demol-

60

ished and the land repossessed for farming. Many squatter sites can still be identified, mostly at the roadside, but the houses now on them were erected by local builders, with the permission of the land owner."[18]

By the last decades of the 20th century just a few people had direct memories of these home-made homes. Ann Wilson, whose father was the water bailiff for the Wrexham and East Denbighshire Water Company in the first decade of the century, whose recollections of the house built by Meg Delf and her late husband on the mountainside at Pen-Y-Cae, seem already to mix folklore with memory.

"Well now, in the beginning Mr Dennis said to them: 'If you can build, put smoke in your chimney before tonight, you can have that piece of ground'. You see, they just built a chimney up you know, part of the outside of the house, and then they had the smoke to come through the chimney. They could have that place for their home and a piece of ground attached to it... The grates then were only like little bars put across, and two little bits of stone at the side, to put the kettle and things like that... And I went with my father, I was only a little girl and I used to go up and collect the rent, ninepence a year."[19]

From the opposite end of the country, in her recollections of a Rhondda childhood, Mary Davies Parnell remembered the weekly walk to Tydraw, over Gelliwion Mountain, past the shack built on the mountain side by Gilo and Anna Vaughan and their ten children, "built of unrendered breeze blocks, bricks and stone, with rusty corrugated sheets for a roof." They were, she recalled, "consequently regarded as gypsies."[20] She herself remembered them as a pleasant enough family.

61

References

1. David Lloyd George "Trusts and Monopolies" (speech in Newcastle, 4 April 1903) printed in *Better Times* (London 1910) cited by R. Merfyn Jones *The North Wales Quarrymen 1874-1922*, Cardiff: University of Wales Press 1982.
2. Oliver Onions *Mushroom Town*, London: Hodder & Stoughton 1914.
3. W.W. Gill "The One-Night House" *Folk-Lore*, September 1944, Vol LV No 3 pp. 128-132.
4. John Williams "Morning and evening surprises" *The Countryman*, Spring 1993, pp. 33-37.
5. *ibid.*
6. Eurwyn William *Home-made Homes: dwellings of the rural poor in Wales*, Cardiff: National Museum of Wales 1988 p.12.
7. *ibid.*
8. John Williams *op cit.*
9. Euryn Wiliam *op cit* p.12.
10. Roger Laidlaw *Community, Work and Religion: mentalities in the villages of the North Wales coalfield c.1930-c.1960*, unpublished Ph.D Thesis, University of Warwick 1995, p.30.
11. *ibid* p.31.
12. *ibid*, citing letter in Clwyd Record Office, Harwarden, DD/4IY/5755.
13. *Report of Inspector of Mines* 1875 (1876) cited by R. Merfyn Jones: *The North Wales Quarryman 1874-1922*, Cardiff: University of Wales Press 1982.
14. R Merfyn Jones *op cit* pp. 25-27.
15. Dennis Griffiths *Out of This Clay*, Clwyd County Library and Information Service, new edition 1992.
16. Roger Laidlaw: *op cit* p.32.
17. J.H. Jones in *Y Brython* 14 July 1919, trans. by Dennis V. Gilpin in his *Rhosllanerchrugog A Volume of Pictures Vol 2*, Wrexham: 1992 and cited in Laidlaw: *op cit* p.55.
18. Jeremy Lowe *Welsh Country Workers Housing 1775-1875*, Cardiff: National Museum of Wales 1985 p.3.
19. Mrs Ann Wilson, taped interview, Wrexham Museum Project 1984
20. Mary Davies Parnell *Block Salt and Candles: a Rhondda childhood*, Bridgend: Poetry Wales Press 1991, pp. 113, 131.

Chapter 6
South-West England and the last one-day house

"The practice of 'squatting' on the moor had not been stopped at the beginning of the nineteenth century. The belief that formerly obtained in regard to it was that if a house could be erected and a piece of land enclosed in a single day between sunrise and sunset, the builder could claim such as his own."

William Crossing: *A Hundred Years on Dartmoor*[1]

Dartmoor, in Devonshire, is a high, bleak and relatively treeless plateau, once famous as a source of tin and copper, and consequently the home of "free miners", capable of manipulating Dartmoor's dense, hard granite.

In the later 19th century Dartmoor had several diligent local historians. One was a Plymouth journalist, William Crossing, another was a celebrated writer, clergyman and collector of folk-lore and folk-song, Sabine Baring-Gould and another was a topographical photographer, Robert Burnard. This is why, by chance, the house called Jolly Lane Cot, at Hexworthy on the West Dart, is so well-recorded. William Crossing explained its history as an example of the belief in the folk-lore of the one-day house, a variant on the one-night house, which he does not discuss. He saw that cottage as the last publicly noticed instance of this procedure. It happened in 1835, when Tom and Sally Satterley built the cottage for Sally's father John, and her step-mother Ann. William Crossing described how, on the day selected for building,

"Everything being in readiness, the labourers of the neighbourhood met on the site, on a day when the farmers, who, as holders of the ancient tenements,

63

Jolly Lane Cottage, Hexworthy.

<u>Top</u> *June 1889. Sally Satterley sitting by the door.* (PHOTO: ROBERT BURNARD).

<u>Bottom</u> *September 1991. The upper floor was added after Mrs Satterley's death in 1901.* (PHOTO: JENNY GOULD).

had rights in the Forest, and would, it was feared, have prevented their plans, had departed to attend Ashburton Fair, Work was commenced, all cheerfully lending assistance. Even before the walls at one end of the house were up, the laying on of the thatch of the roof had begun at the other. By evening all was done, and the 'squatters' were in possession. But this attempt at 'land cribbing' was only partially successful. It is true no ejectment followed, but a small rental was put on the place by the Duchy of Cornwall. The cottage was inhabited until her death in March 1901 by Sally Satterley, the aged widow of its erector, who built it in order to provide a home for his parents."[2]

Robert Burnard, who photographed the house in the 1880s explained that "by nightfall a fire was burning on the hearth and the old couple were safely housed in their new home."[3] The house is there to this day, with another storey added in this century. Mrs Satterley had many of the characteristics that we associate with the builders of informal settlements in the northern hemisphere today. One was her versatility in undertaking every kind of work. William Crossing described admiringly after her death, the way in which she,

"was during the greater part of her life engaged in work usually performed by men. She was for some time employed in the mine at Eylesbarrow, drove pack-horses, could cut peat, was able to mow with a scythe, and as the father of the present Mr Aaron Row of the Duchy Hotel, Princeton, used to say, could nail a shoe to a horse's hoof as well as a blacksmith."[4]

When compiling his pioneer collection of *Songs of the West,* Baring-Gould was told that Mrs Satterley remembered some of the songs that had been sung by her father and on a wild and stormy day drove from Princeton with F.W. Bussell, an Oxford musician, to note down her songs.

"But old Sally could not sit down and sing. We found that the only way in which we could extract the ballade from her was by following her about as she did her usual work. Accordingly we went after her when she fed the pigs, or got sticks from the firewood rick, or filled a pail from the spring, pencil and notebook in hand, jotting down words and melody. Finally she did sit to peel some potatoes, when Mr Bussell with a MS music-book in hand, seated himself on the copper. This position he maintained as she sang the ballad of 'Lord Thomas and the Fair Eleanor', till her daughter applied fire under the cauldron, and Mr Bussell was forced to skip from his perch."[5]

Eric Hemery, in his *High Dartmoor: land and people* described a visit to Sally's great-grandson:

"Miss E.M. Hannaford, who was born at the ancient Tenement of Hexworthy, and now lives in Cornwall, remembers Jolly Lane Cot in its original state and old Sally sitting in the sunshine at her door... The cot is now occupied by Mr Henry Satterley, great-grandson of the redoubtable Sally, who, says Henry, 'could doctor pigs and ponies and do almost anything a man could do.' He showed me recently, how the enlargement of the cot was carried out, in 1901, after Sally's death, into a two storey cottage. The original was thatched with rye-straw on a timber frame; left of the cot was the shippen, divided into three compartments — for pigs, two cows and pony — and beyond it the dairy. Behind the cot are expertly-laid granite steps rising to Acre Field, always rich in grass, and across Jolly Lane is the gate into the garden. All were the work of Tom and Sally."[6]

Humbler homes had been built on the moor and all over Devon, erected, with or without permission, usually from cob, a mixture of clay and straw, and more rarely of granite blocks, and roofed with thatch. In 1808 the agricultural writer Charles Vancouver described the labourers' cottages as of "three mud walls and a hedge bank."[7] Like Mrs Satterley's house, they would have a central door and two rooms, one of which would have a fireplace and a chimney, with a baking oven. The author of *Devon Building* remarks that such houses can be seen anywhere in Devon, even though "such flimsy structures might have stood only for the length of a single generation." He comments that "the basic character of such cottages is soon eroded by modernisation and extensions."[8] However, Jolly Lane Cott is ready to move into another century thanks to this process of continual updating.

As building materials, neither cob and the other variants of clay and chalk, nor stone, are best suited to the building of a house in either a day or a night. The first needs to be put up in 'rises' like brickwork, to allow wet materials to dry, and of course any kind of stone, but especially granite, needs strength and experience in manipulating heavy loads. A Cornish tin-miner, Methodist and poet, John Harris, had a long-term plan to build a house for himself and his family at Troon. Helped by his brother Will (who emigrated to America in 1845) he had cut blocks of granite from Bolenowe in preparation for his house-building. He found a site in Troon and agreed to pay rent once the house was occupied. His biographer, Paul Hewman, explains how he was enabled to start work when he was rewarded with £200 for the discovery of a vein of rich ore in 1846.

"Assisted by his father's horse, Old Golly, he carted stones from the quarry downhill to Troon. Evenings, mornings and sometimes by moonlight too, he shifted the heavy granite blocks for two years, while other miners watched, idly smoking pipes or drinking down their earnings."[9] This model of Methodist sobriety laboured on his house until in March 1848, his family moved in, and in the following spring he began to pay rent to the ground landlord.

There was nothing illicit about John Harris's house, but the Cornish experience of the one-night house has proved a key element in the plot of several romantic novels. In Jean Plaidy's *Lilith*, set in the 18th century, it is explained how:

> "The cottage consisted of one room, and he had built it, with the aid of his friend, during one summer's night, because the law of the land at that time was that anyone who could build a cottage overnight could claim it and the ground on which it stood as his own property."[10]

In *Demelza*, the second of Winston Graham's Poldark novels, set in 1788-1790, a house in north Cornwall is built, not overnight, but over a week-end:

> "First there was the site to be marked; and this must be level enough to support the four walls. They found a patch and cleared it of stones... Then they roughly marked it into a rectangle and began. The walls were to be made of clay, beaten hard and mixed with straw and small stones... a bag of bullock hair... was stirred in with the clay and the stones and the straw to make a building mixture. Four great boulders were used for the corners of the house, and from one to another of these a rough trough was built of wood about two feet wide and two deep. Into this the clay and stones and all the rest were shovelled and stamped down and left to set while more was mixed."[11]

One of Cornwall's historians, A.K. Hamilton Jenkin, asserted that in early 19th century most Cornish houses, especially in the mining areas, were built by the people themselves. He provided a similar account of the quite complicated procedure of building in cob, clay lump and shuttered earth, and described the way that stone and slate were used in those areas where they could be obtained without cost. He also stressed that as every piece of land had a landlord "Such cottages were dumped down anywhere and anyhow wherever a bit of land could be obtained. Some of them still remain in odd corners by the roadsides, or on rock ledges above the fishing coves. Hundreds more were built by the miners amidst the shafts, burrows, and engine-houses of the mines which gave them work."[12] His account of the one-night house stresses the degree of improvisation with a future window opening serving as a temporary chimney, while a hearth and a kind of sleeping attic, called a 'talfat' were subsequently added as the owner's time and income allowed.

In several other books of Cornish life and legends, Hamilton Jenkins returned to this theme, citing another author J.C. Hoare in describing houses built in this way in Cornwall.

"Many of these cottages have been pulled down and new ones erected on the same spot. In other cases new cottages have been built close by, whilst the old one has served for a linhay, or maybe a stable or a cowhouse. Some are actually owned by descendants of the original one-night builders, others again have been sold to the owner of the adjoining land, perhaps in time of want. Not a few have been retaken, but, it would seem, unlawfully, for in quite recent years the Duchy of Cornwall claimed one such cottage, but failed entirely in its suit."[13]

A barrister, Dr Ann Everton, sought in vain for documentary evidence of this case, but, she noted that,

"There is a well-established custom of tin-bounding in the stanneries of Cornwall by which a tin-miner was allowed to mark out any plot on waste ground and mine it, so long as he paid tolls to the owner, but in contrast with this situation, in the custom in issue there is no hint of payment, on the contrary, tho activity grounds a claim of title."[14]

Pursuing her enquiries she found it reported in the 1920s from the West Hill district of Ottery St Mary in Devon that there had been a custom there that:

"...if a man started to build a cottage on waste ground which others claimed (i.e. common land), the objectors were free to pull down during the night what the builder had put up during the day. Once the roof was on, and rain had fallen on it, this privilege lapsed. In consequence, the building was often done at night, and a bit of thatch was put on as soon as possible, and water poured over it. This was held to protect the building from interference."[15]

Following the exploration of the theme of the one-night house in the local newspaper in Somerset, Mr W.W. Gill recorded that:

"the hamlet of Hillcommon near Hilverton is, according to tradition, inhabited by descendants of squatters who at different times, put up their houses in night hours, and by sleeping in them before sunrise, established a legal right. The example was set by a man from Oake named James Hayes, whose dwelling was at first built of turf sods only, and later converted by him into a brick cottage. Other interlopers followed, and thereupon, it is said, legal proceedings were threatened; but they were never enforced."[16]

He also noticed that at Pitsford Hill, three miles from Wiveliscombe on the road to Watchet, there is a house on ground claimed in the 1860s, "after his grindstone had rested there unchallenged for twenty-one years — the period presumed to be requisite in such cases."[17] His final Somerset location was a group of cottages between the road and the river Tone at Athelney in the Somerset Levels. This is a low-lying district devoted to the growing of the withy, the name given to the pliable swift-growing osiers used for making baskets. In most of the villages of the district, the withies were gathered, stripped and bundled and sent away to the basket makers, but Athelney was so isolated that it made sense to export the finished product. Even the guide books are unkind to Athelney. For one it is "a tiny hamlet, dark and damp"[18] and for another, "the scene is uninspiring at the best of times, and is peculiarly dreary in the winter."[19]

But Athelney provided a variant on the conditions for legitimising a one-night house. Mr Gill found that, "At this place a lightly-covered structure of hurdles was thought sufficient to comply with the unwritten law."[20]

In the less remote villages of Somerset, the submerged history of squatter houses is being explored with examination of estate records and the surviving evidence on, or in, the ground, by the Somerset and South Avon Vernacular Building Research Group which has published its studies on a growing series of villages, studying the homes of the gentry, yeomen and husbandmen, lesser farmers, craftsmen and labourers. The Group's report, for example, on the houses, cottages and farms of Chiselborough, records that the last of the categories of inhabitants, the labourers, were

"the cottagers (or squatters) who built on the lord's waste and who also enclosed parts of the waste for gardens or orchards. One such labourer, Lionell Still, 'a poore man and had many children, and noe house to succor him and his famylie' petitioned Sir Edward Hext at the general Sessions at Ilchester in 1614 to allow a relaxation of the 'Cottages Act' of

1589 to give him a licence to erect a house 'in some wast plott apoynted by the officers and parishioners'. His request was supported by fourteen prominent parishioners, and having already received the leave of the Lady of the Manor, was successful... Other people were probably encouraged by Still's success and subsequently many other squatter cottages were built, An Estate Survey in 1742 states that there were eleven and the 1808 Survey lists twenty-two... Estate Surveys up to the early 19th century acknowledged that they paid no rent but later they paid 10s per year."[21]

There is no reason to suppose that the homes of squatters were any less fit for habitation than those provided by farmers for their workers. In his account of Victorian village life, Neil Philip cites an account from 1874 of cottages at Montacute, Somerset distinguished by their "chilling air of misery and wretchedness":

"The one bedroom over the stone floor apartment was a kind of attic, almost entirely denuded of furniture. There was a window on each side. But several panes of the glass had been broken, and the holes stuffed with rags. In this one small wretched apartment, in some parts of which I could not have stood upright, the eight persons composing this family had to sleep — father, mother and six children. The mother told me that at one time the family living at home consisted of no less than thirteen persons, who all had to sleep in the one small bedroom of the cottage."[22]

And yet "this village was renowned for the prosperity of its farmers, the land in the district being some of the richest in the whole country."[23] Further up country in Wiltshire, J.H. Bettey has traced the evolution of overnight cottages that survived. He cites the court rolls of the manor of

Cranborne, where in 1625 some of the tenants complained to the Earl of Salisbury's steward that a poor labourer, Richard Cooke

> "intends either this night or the next to set up a house (which he hath already framed) upon the common of Alderholt, and hath placed straw upon the common in the place he hath made choyce of to erect his house in...' In this instance the tenants objected because they claimed that the number of squatters who were already established on the common was so great that the common grazing-land available for their cattle was severely restricted, and they wished to stop any further encroachments."[24]

He notes how the county has many other examples of the establishment of similar squatters' settlements, resisted in places where manorial control was strictly enforced, but in the claylands and heaths where tracts of common or ancient woodland remained, "many such communities came into existence" with "the inhabitants making their living by day labour in agriculture or industry and gradually acquiring a right to their cottages only because manorial authorities, either through negligence or because they needed the labour, turned a blind eye to their existence." Mr Bettey describes a series of examples:

> "A survey of Kingston Lacy made in 1591 listed 30 cottages recently built on the waste and heathland there; and in 1598 the Commissioners of the Duchy of Lancaster complained that one Thomas Chater had enclosed an acre of the heath at Holt Forest and had erected a cottage there 'at a place called Crooked Wythes... which is verie inconvenient, as well for the spoyling of the deere as for the spoyling of the woods and otherwise.' In spite of these complaints the cottage survived and still stands today in its acre enclosure at Crooked Wythies...

"A good example of such a squatters' community grew up on the waste-land at the edge of Warminster Common in Wiltshire, in an area of heath and woodland well away from the town. During the seventeenth century a few small cottages were built there and in spite of half-hearted attempts by the Longleat estate to prevent the growth of the settlement, other squatters' hovels were erected during the eighteenth century. By 1791 there were more than 1,000 people living there in some 200 cottages and hovels..."[25]

Reflecting on the situation of the Dorsetshire labourer and his family, Thomas Hardy concluded that the cottager whose home was not dependent on his job was happier, regardless of the quality of his cottage. For "it must be remembered that melancholy among the rural poor arises primarily from a sense of the incertitude and precariousness of their position." He found that

"Copyholders, cottage freeholders, and the like, are as a rule less trim and neat, more muddling in their ways, than the dependent labourer; and yet there is no more comfortable or serene being than the cottager who is sure of his roof."[26]

When he was asked to comment on the Dorsetshire Labourer in the context of rural depopulation in the 1880s, he referred especially to those cottagers who were not farm workers — the blacksmith, the carpenter, the shoe-maker, the small higgler, the shopkeeper:

"Many of these families had been life-holders, who built, at their own expense, the cottages they occupied, and as the lives dropped, and the property fell in, they would have been glad to remain as weekly or monthly tenants of the owner. But the policy of all but some few philanthropic landowners is to disapprove of these petty tenants who are not in the estate's employ, and to pull down each cottage as it fall is, leaving standing a sufficient number for the use of the farmer's men and no more. But the question of the Dorset cottager here merges in that of all the houseless and landless poor, and the vast topic of the Rights of Man, to consider which is beyond the scope of a merely descriptive article."[27]

The historian of the rural poor, Keith Snell, devotes a chapter to the experiences of the Dorset labourer that Hardy failed to mention, even at the turn of the century, when asked by a fellow novelist Rider Haggard, who had been asked to report to the government of the day on the same theme of rural depopulation.[28] Snell describes how, apart from unemployment and low wages and the appalling way farm labourers were treated by their employers,

"Cottage building was far behind by the 1830s, and remained so until very late in the nineteenth century. In many parishes, cottages remained the squalid mud huts they had been in 1843, when it was reported to a parliamentary commission that 'In nine villages out of ten the cottage is still nothing but a slightly improved hovel.'"[29]

A vital topic that Hardy had observed was the way that it had been common for Dorset farmers, on horseback amidst a field of workers, to "address them with a contemptuousness which could not have been greatly exceeded in the days when the thralls of Cedric wore their collars of brass."[30] And over a century later an elderly labourer recalled how "However much you worked and scrambled, the farmers just wiped their boots on you."[31]

In this sense Hardy had been right to discern that, even the squalor that was the plight of the independent cottager was less hopeless than that of the labouring family in a tied cottage. When legal housing was appalling, illicit housing was no worse.

References

1. William Crossing *A Hundred Years on Dartmoor*, Plymouth: Western Morning News 1901. New edition, edited by Brian Le Messurier, Newton Abbot: David and Charles 1967. p.32.
2. *ibid* p.90.
3. Robert Burnard *Dartmoor Pictorial Records*, privately printed 1890.
4. William Crossing *op cit* p.90.
5. S. Baring-Gould *A Book of Dartmoor*, 1890. Cited in Eric Hemery, below
6. Eric Hemery *High Dartmoor: land and people*, London: Robert Hale 1983 p.412.
7. C. Vancouver *General View of the Agriculture of the County of Devon*, 1808, reprinted by David and Charles 1969.
8. Peter Beacham (ed) *Devon Building*, Exeter: Devon Books 1990.
9. Paul Newman *The Meads of Love: the life and poetry of John Harris (1820-84)*. (Still awaiting publication).
10. Jean Plaidy *Lilith*, London: Robert Hale 1954. p.13.
11. Winston Graham *Demelza*, London: Werner Laurie 1946. Fontana 1968. pp. 76-77.
12. A.K. Hamilton Jenkin *The Story of Cornwall*, London: Thomas Nelson 1934.
13. J.C. Hoare "Quaint Houses in Cornwall" in *Old Cornwall* No 6, 1927, cited in A.K. Hamilton Jenkin *Cornwall and its People*, London: J.M. Dent 1945, new edition Newton Abbot: David & Charles 1988, p.326.
14. Ann R. Everton: "Built in a Night." in *The Conveyancer and Property Lawyer* Vol XXXV: 1971 pp. 249-254.
15. *Devon and Cornwall Notes and Queries* Vol XIV, Pt 2 April 1926, cited by Everton *op cit*.
16. W.W. Gill: "The One-Night House" *Folk-Lore* September 1944, Vol LV, No 3. pp. 128-132, where he explains that "these matters were ventilated in the Local Notes and Queries columns of the *Somerset County Herald* at the junction of 1938 and 1939."
17. *ibid*.
18. M. Lovell Turner: *Somerset*, London: Robert Hale 1949.
19. G.M. Wade: *Rambles in Somerset*, London: Methuen 1923 p.267.

20. W.W. Gill *op cit.*
21. Somerset & South Avon Vernacular Building Research Group *Somerset Villages: the house, cottages and farms of Chiselborough*, (SSAVBRG, c/o Somerset Rural Life Museum Abbey Farm, Chilkwell Road, Glastonbury, Somerset BA5 8DB, 1993).
22. Neil Philip *Victorian Village Life*, London: Albion 1993, p.77, quoting Francis George Heath *The English Peasantry*, London: Frederick Warne 1874.
23. *ibid* p.78.
24. J.H. Bettey *Rural Life in Wessex 1500-1900*, (1977) Gloucester: Alan Sutton 1987 p.57.
25. *ibid* pp. 57-59.
26. Thomas Hardy "The Dorsetshire Labourer" *Longmans Magazine* Vol 21 July 1883, pp. 252-269, p.256 (Reprinted in J. Moynahan (ed) *The Portable Thomas Hardy* 1977).
27. *ibid* p.269.
28. H. Rider Haggard *The Poor and the Land*, London: Longmans, Green 1905.
29. K.D.M. Snell *Annals of the Labouring Poor: social change and England 1660-1900*, Cambridge University Press 1985 p.380.
30. Thomas Hardy *ibid*.
31. cited in B. Kerr *Bound to the Soil: a social history of Dorset, 1750-1918*, 1968.

Plump Hill, Gloucestershire: an encroachment or squatters' settlement on the edge of the Forest of Dean. The cottages and tiny enclosures are interspersed with old quarries, iron mines and lime kilns. (PHOTO: PAUL COONES)

Chapter 7
Deep in the forest

"The only good purpose that these forests answer is that of furnishing a place of being to labourers' families on their skirts; and here their cottages are very neat, and the people are hearty and well, just as they do round the forest of Hampshire. Every cottage has a pig or two. These graze in the forest, and, in the fall, eat acorns and beech-nuts and the seed of the ash; for, these last, as well as the others, are very full of oil, and a pig that is put to his shifts will pick the seed very nicely out from the husks. Some of these foresters keep cows, and all of them have bits of ground, cribbed, of course, at different times, from the forest, and to what better use can the ground be put?"

William Cobbett *Rural Rides*[1]

Royal parks and forests are famous for their squatters, possibly because they were eventually subject to a less vigilant system of supervision than other parts of the country. When first seized by the Norman kings (although the Anglo-Saxon kings already had hunting parks) they were surrounded with punitive laws against poaching and trespass. Hands were chopped off and eyes put out. By medieval times royal forests "may have covered up to 30 per cent of England."[2] But a series of concessions were made in the 13th century. One historian of the New Forest, explains that "the rigour of forest law was mitigated in the days of Henry III, the whole of whose charter of the forests is framed against the annoyance which the inhabitants had felt from the severity of the former laws" and granted "privileges which were probably the origin of many 'forest rights' now claimed in the district."[3]

Lesser landlords with their own rivalries with the sovereign are more diligent on their own behalf than on his. The 19th century American traveller Washington Irving remarked that,

"I have often observed that the more proudly a mansion has been tenanted in the day of its prosperity, the humbler are its inhabitants in the days of its decline, and that the palace of a king commonly ends in being the nestling-place of the beggar. The Alhambra is in a rapid state of similar transition. Whenever a tower falls to decay, it is seized upon by some tatterdemalion family, who become joint tenants, with the bats and owls, of its gilden halls..."[4]

English royalty was usually less hard-pressed, but a Victorian historian of Windsor Castle recalled that at one time "paupers had squatted in many of the towers"[5] and in the early 19th century Ann Hicks, an apple woman, annexed a portion of Hyde Park at the east end of the Serpentine. Her shanty was known as the White Cottage, and Mr H. Askew explained its gradual growth:

"from a stall with an awning a lock-up shop was evolved. Then a small back enclosure appeared including four walls with windows and a door. The height of the building was next increased and under the excuse of repairing the roof a chimney was provided. The next step was to get a hurdle erected to prevent the curious from peering in at the window. The fence by degrees was moved outwards until a fair amount of space was enclosed. At this stage the authorities interfered and secured possession of the domain of Ann Hicks who was granted a small allowance."[6]

The same technique of enlargement was reported by the author of Ward Lock's guide to the New Forest, describing the cottage holdings at Hill Top, East Boldre and Beaulieu Rails on the forest fringe where "The inside of the hedge was cut, and the briars and stuff thrown outside. These shot out and formed a sort of rolling fence, and so the would-be squatters kept trimming the inside and adding to the outside." Like Cobbett, this observer admired the self-sufficiency and independence of the New Forest squatters and their "singular combination of reticence and self-possession, with good humour and friendliness."[7] A similar settlement on the western edge of the forest is to this day called Nomansland. Life in the squatter cottages of a New Forest parish is contrasted with life in the slums of a Victorian industrial city in Elizabeth Gaskell's 1855 novel *North and South*,[8] and at the end of the century an old resident, C.J. Cornish, provided a history of the forest, with a detailed account of the folklore of the one-night house:

"A favourite site for their colonies was on the fringe of some great estate projecting into the Crown Forest. At Beaulieu, for instance, the boundary of the property is called the 'Manor Bank.' South and east of the Abbey it abuts on high flat open heaths; and there the line of division is a bank in the literal sense, a high rampart of earth separating the cultivated land and plantations of Beaulieu from the wild and open forest. To this bank, the cottages of the commoners and squatters cling like swallows' nests to the eaves. It is said that in the old days of encroachments, custom ruled that if a house were once built, roofed, and a fire lit within, it was not in the power of the Crown to put it down. Occupation, and not architecture, was the object of the squatters, and the game of house-building in the forest was soon played with a skill born of long practice which baffled the spasmodic fits of energy on the part of the authorities. It reached such a stage of perfection that the art of building, roofing, putting in a chimney, and lighting a fire within the space of a single winter's night was at last attained; and the curl of smoke rising defiantly in the grey of a December morning was the signal that the squatter had triumphed, and that henceforth he was irremovable."[9]

Echoing Elizabeth Gaskell's observation of the way in which "a squatter's roughly-built and decaying cottage had disappeared" and "a new one, tidy and respectable, had been built in its stead", Cornish went on to describe how

"Some of these little cabins are still used, though more commodious dwellings have been added to them. Others stand, or are tumbling down, in the gardens of later buildings. Fifty years of settled and prosperous occupation have not given them the complacency of the humdrum cottage. They never quite lose the hasty, half-defiant look which is their birthmark, though their present owners enjoy a degree of security, independence, and general goodwill, which their honourable and industrious lives fully justify."[10]

He explained that the cottages at Hill Top are set in narrow, fertile strips of garden won from the poor soil of Beaulieu Heath, and have walls of cob or clay-lump, and roofs of straw-thatch, sometimes replaced by slats. They have been transformed again in the twentieth century by prosperity and the tourist trade which brings eight million visitors to the New Forest every year. At the Visitors' Centre we learn about the function of the forest as a source of timber, as there is no record of any sovereign hunting there after James II. The guide explains that

"Since the unfortunate peasants who dwelt in the Forest were forbidden to enclose their land lest any fence should interfere with the free run of the deer, their domestic animals were allowed to graze by common right and browse through the Forest and this grazing reinforced by that of the deer themselves, severely diminished the ability of the sparse woodlands to perpetuate themselves. The way was thus clear for the passing of the Deer Removal Act of 1851, under which the deer were ordered to be destroyed and in return the Crown was authorised to enclose and plant a further 10,000 acres. It subsequently proved impossible to remove the deer, but these new Inclosures aroused considerable opposition from the commoners, whose cattle still grazed the Open Forest."[11]

Visitors can still encounter deer of several species, as well as New Forest ponies and the grazing animals of the commoners who retain their rights of *estover* or firewood gathering, *turbary* or peat-cutting, and *pannage*, allowing pigs to forage for beech-mast and acorns in the autumn. Two thirds of the 144 square miles of the forest still belongs to the Crown and is administered by the Forestry Commission. Much of the privately-owned third belongs to the Montagu family, descendants of one of the illegitimate children of Charles II. And as Paul Barker observes sharply, "The biggest industry in the New Forest is heritage, a replicated past feeding our voracious curiosity."[12]

The other great hunting forest that was outside the usual modes of land tenure was the Forest of Dean in Gloucestershire between the rivers Severn and Wye. It expanded and contracted from Saxon times onward, with the fortunes of monarchs and early in the nineteenth century its boundaries were fixed around an area of about 23,000 acres. The visitor is immediately struck by the absence of historic settlement of any description. The forest

"with its own laws and customs was effectively isolated from many of the forces which fashioned the landscape elsewhere. Only in the manors on the edge of this exclusively royal playground, deliberately maintained as waste, did nucleated settlements grow up around medieval churches in anything approaching a conventional fashion. The Church did not gain a foothold in the forest proper until much later, when squatting led to the establishment of encroachments with growing populations. Then... this 'desolate, extra-parochial tract of land... came to be dominated, as was the South Wales coalfield, by 'Chapel' rather than 'Church.'"[13]

Unlike the New Forest, the Forest of Dean had other resources beyond timber and subsistence food production. The smelting of iron ore, and consequently charcoal-burning were important from Roman times until the 17th century, after which time, coal-mining became the dominant industry until late in the 20th century. Natives of the forest are known as foresters, and among them are the free miners, who are awarded the right to work 'gales' or places to extract coal or iron by a Crown official, the Gaveller. A forest historian, Humphrey Phelps, explains that "To become a free miner a man had to be born within the Hundred of St Brievals and to have worked for a year and a day in an iron or coal mine within the Hundred."[14] He explains the absence of buildings of architectural merit, in the forest:

"By the time of encroachments, when settlements were established and churches were needed, the art of architecture, as opposed to mere building, had been lost. Before that time there had been squatters; the forester believed he had the right to build so long as he got smoke going up the chimney before nightfall on the day that he built his cottage or cabin. If fortunate he stayed, if unlucky he was evicted."[15]

84

He quotes an earlier historian explaining that "Cromwell expelled nearly 400 cabins of beggarly people, living upon the waste and destroying the wood and timber. In 1680 about 30 cabins had again been erected, which were demolished, with the enclosures about them"[16] However, towards the end of the 18th century there was a steady repopulation, and "in 1803 the number of houses had increased to 696, and there were 662 free miners recorded in the forest. Ten years later the area of encroachment amounted to 1,600 acres divided into over 2,000 patches with 785 houses inhabited by 1,111 people."[17]

In the early 19th century, a long series of confrontations and skirmishes between the agents of the Crown and the foresters and free miners brought an end to their independence. In the time of Charles I, the King hoped to ease his financial problems by leasing the whole Forest to an ambitious ironwork's owner, Sir John Winter. This involved the land, the trees, the mines and quarries. Winter felled a huge quantity of trees and fenced 4,000 acres for regrowth. But the foresters continually pulled down the fences. The threat in the period 1800 to 1841 was more serious. Chris Fisher, the historian of the free miners, is eloquent about the meaning of those years:

"Over that period the State and Capital together broke down the old system in Dean, under which the miners, through the operation of their Mine Law Court, the exclusive right of 'free mining' which the Kings of England had allowed them time out of mind, and the laxity and venality of Crown officials had been able to base their lives on small scale, independent proprietorship of land and mines and the harvesting of the Forest. From about 1800 the body of custom and right which had governed Dean came to be seen as outdated and inconvenient, as a threat to the security of property and the interest of the State, defined with new emphasis by 'economical' and administrative reform. The majority of free miners became wage workers, their industry passed into the hands of strangers and the uses they had made of the forest were outlawed."[18]

He describes the way the forest had provided its inhabitants with a rich, but unprotected economic resource, it "offered timber, wood and bark, coal, iron ore and limestone, building stone, deer, apples, herbs and open space for cottages and gardens", while lax Crown control allowed them to build these cottages, "mostly made of stone but also of wood, turf, mud and rush", and to enclose gardens and orchards, "and to take the bark, herbs and timber for their own use and profit." And, listing these assets he concludes that

"since the Forest was extra-parochial Crown land, there were no rates or taxes to pay, no schools or schoolmasters, no Churches or ministers, no soldiers or constables or large scale employers. This, however rough and inadequate it is, is a sketch of a community of small proprietors who had a considerable degree of independence and freedom from authority."[19]

Chris Fisher explains that all through the 19th century a succession of Crown officials, Commissioners, Capitalists, Speculators, Preachers and Teachers marched through the Forest as "bearers of some innovating principle by which they could re-organise life there and the ways in which resources were to be used and controlled." The royal interest in the forest was administered through two hierarchies, that of the Surveyor General of Woods and Forests, concerned with ensuring a supply of timber for the naval dockyards, and the Constable of the Castle of St Briavels whose task was to collect for the Crown a fifth share of the produce of the mines. The free miners dug shallow pits and drift mines or 'levels' with an ascending passage cut into the hillside to reach a coal seam. By the

1830s the rights of the free miners had been eroded and 'foreigners' using capital to mine on a far larger scale with waged labour provided a far greater revenue for the Crown, but encroachers still occupied land "and defied attempts to bring them to acknowledge that title to the land lay in the Crown."[20]

In 1830 Warren James, "a native and free miner of the Hundred of St Briavels", petitioned against a Bill confirming the gradual enclosure of the Forest by the Commissioners. One morning in June that year

"James and about eighty others began to break down the fences, ignoring two readings of the Riot Act by magistrates. About 300 people joined them by the end of the first day, including eighty women who 'seemed more intent on the work of destruction than the men'. The mob grew to between two and three thousand people. They remained in control of the forest for four days and levelled about sixty miles of fence, hedge and embankment. They breached most of the enclosures in some way and in a number of places drove cattle and swine in to graze on the undergrowth and acorns. In parties of fifty to three hundred the rioters worked in an orderly and disciplined manner, 'in much the same way as they would have worked at anything else.' They were 'civil in their deportment' and 'offered no personal violence and indeed confined themselves wholly to the destruction of the fences'. James, indeed, 'sent for a constable and in his presence superintended the work of destruction, observing that he had sent for him to keep the peace.'"[21]

Warren James had assured his supporters that "not only the King but the Duke of Beaufort is on our side — he is the poor man's friend and will see us righted," but on the following Sunday, the Dragoons, with swords drawn and followed by the Duke of Beaufort and other magistrates and gentlemen, galloped into Coleford, while "the rioters offered no resistance but scattered to hide in the woods and coal pits." Eventually seven men were given prison sentences and Warren James was given a death sentence but was, instead, transported to New South Wales for life. "In 1838, after the Mines Act had passed safely onto the statute books His Majesty pardoned Warren James, but no news of him or from him ever came back to the forest."[22]

There followed a series of concessions to the foresters. Although the Commissioners had argued that the inhabitants had no right of common, they withdrew from this, admitting the right to graze pigs and sheep. They also agreed to pass freeholds to the occupiers and to make all conveyances under the Act free of legal expenses and stamp duty.

Later in the century the issues that the foresters thought had been settled in the 1830s were raised again, and, as Chris Fisher put it, "The land question became an important, though muddled, local political issue. It became a focus of Liberal and Conservative competition for votes in the forest division and it became the means by which the Crown hoped to strip away the vestiges of the foresters' rights. It proved, however, that the foresters would not give up the rights."[23]

But the government withdrew its Dean Forest Bill as a result of the intervention of the Commons Preservation Society (now the Open Spaces Society) which had been founded in 1865. The Society's secretary, G. Shaw Lefevre, successfully approached the government to urge that just as it had declared "the intention to preserve the New Forest open and uninclosed, for the benefit of the Commoners and the public enjoyment" so the Forest of Dean was not unworthy of the same treatment. He went on,

"I also pointed out that there could be no reason why a different policy should be pursued in respect of the two forests; that both of them in their present condition were valuable legacies to the nation; that if reduced into absolute ownership of the Crown, they could not be recovered; while, so long as they were subject to Commoners' rights, they could from time to time be adapted to every necessary want, such as that now existing in the Forest of Dean for sites for miners' houses and for allotments without depriving them of their value for public enjoyment and recreation."[24]

This view was accepted without argument by the government of the day.

The Forest of Dean has escaped the explosion of tourism that has overtaken the New Forest. Its straggling villages have no historic churches. It is a different world from the neighbouring Cotswolds. Its best-known writers, the late Dennis Potter and Winifred Foley, stress the Forest's isolation and its consequent curiosities of dialect.[25]

When Dennis Potter grew up in the Forest, the needs of the post war decade had made every ton of coal vital. This brought full employment to the colliers and wider horizons for their children. In 1958, when he revisited parents and neighbours in the pubs, clubs and chapels, the National Coal Board was already closing down all the uneconomic pits, leaving the bitterness later felt in every mining area. The surviving free miners, crouching in their tunnels, patiently explained to him "the virtues of being craftsmen working to their own pace and their own needs, cruelly hard on some days, but more relaxed on others."[26]

Among the hills of the Herefordshire edge of the forest, the site of open-cast mining on a small scale, J.W. Tonkin found "a no-man's-land of narrow, often unsurfaced lanes, a real maze, with little houses built by the miners of 150 and 200 years ago."[27] And when Humphrey Phelps explored the forest he met a man digging in his garden in the valley between Blakeney and Viney Hill with its old quarry. "They do say," the man told him, "that two sisters carried the stone from this quarry to build their house."[28]

References

1. William Cobbett *Rural Rides*, Everyman Edition, London: J.M. Dent 1912. i.p.29.
2. Paul Coones & John Patten *The Penguin Guide to the Landscape of England and Wales*, Harmondsworth: Penguin Books 1986. p.161.
3. C.J. Cornish *The New Forest and The Isle of Wight,* London: Seeley 1895. p.8.
4. Washington Irving *The Alhambra*, (1832) London: Macmillan 1896 p.91.
5. William Hepworth Dixon *Royal Windsor Vol 4*, London: Hurst & Blackett 1879.
6. H. Askew in *Notes and Queries* 30 July 1932, Vol clxii, p.85.
7. *Ward Lock's Illustrated Guide to the New Forest*, London: Ward Lock 1905 p.81.
8. Elizabeth Gaskell *North and South*, (1855) Oxford: World's Classics. 1998.
9. C.J. Cornish *op cit* p.74.
10. *ibid* p.75.
11. Donn Small and John Chapman *Explore the New Forest: an official guide*, London: HMSO 1987 p.10.
12. Paul Barker "Observations" *New Statesman* 17 April 1998, p.54.
13. Paul Coones & John Patten *op cit* pp. 187-8.
14. Humphrey Phelps *The Forest of Dean*, Gloucester: Alan Sutton 1982 p.10.
15. *ibid* p.17.
16. *ibid* p.18, citing Rudge's *History of Gloucestershire*, 1803.
17. *ibid* p.18.
18. Chris Fisher "The Free Miners of the Forest of Dean 1800-1841" in Royden Harrison (ed) *The Coal Miner as Archetypal Proletarian Reconsidered*, Hassocks, Sussex: The Harvester Press 1978 (pp. 17-55) p.17.
19. *ibid* p.25.
20. *ibid* p.37.
21. *ibid* p.40.
22. *ibid* p.41, citing *The Life of Warren James. By a Resident Forester* (Monmouth 1831)
23. Chris Fisher *Custom, Work and Market Capitalise: the Forest of Dean colliers 1788-1888*, London: Croom Helm 1981.
24. G. Shaw Lefevre of the Commons Preservation Society, cited by Fisher, *op cit*.
25. Winifred Foley *A Child in the Forest*, London: BBC 1974, Dennis Potter *The Changing Forest*, (1958) London:

Minerva 1996.

26. Dennis Potter *ibid* p.35.
27. J.W. Tonkin *Herefordshire*, London: B.T. Batsford 1977 p.30.
28 Humphrey Phelps *op cit* p.52.

Chapter 8
At home in Herefordshire

"We stopped to look at the stone of the ruined village pound. With a touch of dry humour the Mayor told us that at the last Court Leet the village authorities and tenants of the Manor had made a present to the Lord of the Manor of the pound, the stop gate and the village well, that he might keep them in repair. Pointing to one of his fields, whose boundary had lately been moved and enlarged, he said with a merry twinkle in his eye, 'Because the Lord had not land enough before, I have taken in a bit more for him off the waste'."

Francis Kilvert *Kilvert's Diary*[1]

Herefordshire, on the Welsh borders, is traditionally a county of pastureland, orchards and hop-gardens, punctuated by the river Wye and its tributaries. The river forms its western boundary with Radnorshire and Brecknockshire, passing through Hay-on-Wye. The Rev. Francis Kilvert whose diaries from the 1870s were discovered and published by William Plomer at the end of the 1930s, was the curate at Clyro on the Welsh side, and then the vicar of Bredwardine in Herefordshire, parishes with identical characteristics.

Kilvert, as part of his parochial duties, visited the rich in their great houses and the poor in their hovels, although Plomer noted that perhaps in our own day, "a man of Kilvert's sensitiveness would be more troubled by the contrast between the bad housing and misery of the very poor and the pleasant junketings of the leisured class"[2], but he did visit one squatter cottage that shocked him, because it housed a solitary, or hermit, who was a fellow-clergyman. His little grey hut "was built of rough dry stone without mortar and the thatch was thin and broken. At one end of the cabin a little garden had been enclosed and fenced in from the waste."[3]

A century after Kilvert, another explorer of the Wye valley, J.W. Tonkin, noted on Byford Common "a typical collection of late, timber-framed, squatters' houses"[14] and at the western end of Breinton, close to the Wye, he found

> "haphazard commons development of the late seventeenth century onwards, tiny houses, some timber-framed, some brick, which have 'just growed' and many of which are still along muddy lanes away from the surfaced road. The area is now changing rapidly as these houses of an earlier poor are bought and modernised by twentieth-century Herefordians."[5]

The architectural historian James Moir has explored the evolution of no fewer than ninety-six squatter settlements that had sprouted on Herefordshire's commons by the 1840s, in a wonderfully exhaustive model of research into local archives and the local press and police records.[6] The details he was able to excavate enabled him to put into perspective the kind of derogatory comments made about squatter communities. I mentioned in my account of Welsh squatter settlements the opinions collected in 1844 by the Select Committee on Enclosure, which displayed an implacable hostility toward squatters. James Moir sees their report as a goldmine of contemporary attitudes:

> "While virtually every moral failing was levelled at those resident on the commons by the witnesses — the Rev. Jones for example simply dismissed them as 'the most immoral and worst portion of the rural population' — criminal activity, drunkenness and idleness, sexual promiscuity and religious indifference stand out for their repetitiveness. On criminal activity, Mr H. Crawter thought that 'the unenclosed commons are invariably nurseries for petty

94

crime; on idleness and drunkeness he believed 'the wives and families are in a state of destitution from the dissolute habits of the men'; Mr Keen thought that 'the population on the verge of these commons are not to be compared, in point of usefulness to society, to labourers who are not on the verge of commons' while Robert Fuller Graham remarked 'I think the beer-shop is maintained by them.' He also ventured comments on their promiscuity: 'their families 'are so large that they all live together, as it were, in one bed', and on their religious indifference and lack of education: 'you rarely find cottagers residing on a common who frequent any place of worship; it is with greatest difficulty in the world you can prevail upon them to send their children to school'."[7]

To assess the validity of this general impression of squatter areas, Moir examines the detailed police records for one year, 1862, from the Dore Division which comprised 23 parishes in the south-west of the county, covering the Black Mountain foothills. From the evidence, he found that,

"The striking features regarding this reputedly dissolute region are firstly the low level and general pettiness of the crimes committed, and secondly the favourable light the commoners appear in when compared to other sections of the population. Poaching and sheep-stealing do register, but the unremarkable figures serve to show that, contrary to the belief of outsiders, not all poachers or sheep-stealers were squatters (and vice versa); indeed, there is some contrary evidence to suggest that given the difficulties of detection with this kind of crime, the rural police force were sometimes 'programmed' wrongly to suspect those whose cottages bordered the commons."[8]

He made a similar examination of bequests in the wills of commoners, "an excellent source for exploding many of the beliefs held by outsiders concerning the squatters' supposed indulgence in moral vices of every kind." What he found of course was the way in which "bequests often reveal affectionate reciprocal bonds within the family and deep concern for the future welfare of individual members" as well as the incidental evidence of "a strong belief in moral justice and correct behaviour." But he warns us of the danger of substituting one myth for another, since "because of the timeless quality of myth, each approach entirely excludes the possibility of change."[9]

Moir seeks similarly to understand the mythology of the folklore of the one-night house, which is as prevalent in the border counties as in Wales. As long ago as 1799, Charles Heath was writing in *The Excursion down the Wye from Ross to Monmouth* that a Mr Shaw had asserted that in the area around the Wye, "he saw a small hut, by the water side, carelessly heaped together, which according to established custom, the indigent natives raise in the night; this, if they can accomplish it, so as to cover in, and boil a pot, within the space of twelve hours unmolested, becomes their own; and they are allowed to enclose a sufficient quantity of land around it, and to rebuild a more suitable cottage." However, Heath cites this opinion only to refute it, with the view that "Mr Shaw was wrongfully informed... The best authority warrants me in saying that no such privilege exists... The land-owner can eject by process of the Court Baron, and if the settler refuses to take notice, proceedings more summary can be had against him."[10]

But Herefordshire provided examples of local variants on the folklore of the one night house. A history of Bromyard compiled by local residents in 1955 described the Downs outside the village, where,

"The cottages in the area are mostly built of grey limestone from a local quarry. It is said that, at one

96

time, anyone wishing to clear a site for building would mark out an area by boundary fires which they kept alight all night — if they were not turned off in twenty-four hours, they kept the land and built their cottages."[11]

When Ann Everton gathered this account, she remarked that she could find no other example in Britain of "so dramatic, and, significantly, by no means secret, a method of acquiring land", but did find an analogy in the history of the settlement of Iceland by Norwegians during the ninth and tenth centuries. There, rules were determined to prevent people from appropriating unlimited land, by marking the outer limits with two fires.[12] In the early 20th century, when Ella Leather was gathering *The Folklore of Herefordshire* she was told that "on Ruckhall Common, people used to come in a night and put up a hut of the roughest kind. By lighting a fire from which smoke would rise before daybreak, this was sufficient to establish a right to the site, and squatters would build a better house on the same plot of ground at their leisure."[13]

For James Moir there is significance in the regional variations in reports of the myth of the one-night house in different parts of the country. "In Cornwall and Wales, the entire house had to be standing by daybreak; in Devon, notional completion appears to have sufficed in that 'a bit of thatch was put on', while in Herefordshire and Shropshire only a chimney, either erected and complete in the former or smoking by dawn in the latter was required." Similarly most of the examples that are told of the one-night house refer to the west of the country. "The lack of examples from the east would tend to point to the more depressed state of the labouring poor in that region, with an intermediate region on the Welsh border where the emphasis on property rights rather than simply a dwelling-place suggests a difference in status between the claimants to the east and west of the border..."

97

He reminds us that, strictly speaking, the term 'squatter' implies only "those inhabitants who had encroached their parcel of waste, had erected on it a cottage or house, and had then sat tight undisturbed and uninterrupted for twenty years (the period prescribed by the Statute of Limitations for gaining full or freehold possession). Not surprisingly, no figures are available demonstrating the success rate of this method." Similarly the concrete evidence for the frequency of the one-night house is rather sparse, and "indeed, not a single reference in a legal document has been found." He suggests, however, that "The myth tried to condense into a night what should have effectively by statute taken twenty years."[14]

Moir describes "the increasing resource by Herefordshire squatters to legalistic devices, such as wills and landsales, and to the law courts to challenge the claims of the manor or vestry over their encroachments, conversely becomes a measure of the relative slackening of outside control, and is accompanied by greater vocal support for the plight of the squatter who by the early nineteenth century is increasingly depicted as being subject to the whims of oppressive, grasping landlords." And he provides examples to show how wills were seen by squatters as surrogate title deeds: "a minute attention to the locality of land enclosed out of the commons coupled with details of length of possession or mode of inheritance demonstrate that the act of will-making was regarded by squatters as a means of leaving *written* proof of their rights to the land."

In examining squatter settlements around the middle of the 19th century and the impact of both piecemeal and Parliamentary enclosures, James Moir divided the county into five areas. The first is the Central Plain: the cluster of lowland parishes at the base of the county's 'bowl' shape. The second is the Eastern Region bordering mainly on Worcestershire and the Malvern Hills and to the south, the Forest of Dean. The third is the Ross region in the south-east of the county, bordering on Gloucestershire and Gwent, the fourth is the South-West region, sharing the Black Mountains with Radnorshire in Wales and the fifth is the Scarplands region in the North-West of the county.

In each of these regions the characteristics of common land determined the pattern of squatter cottages. In parts of the Central Plain Region some parishes have numerous small commons, and in some of them "the concentration of squatter settlement on only one of the commons can be so striking as to suggest that it had virtually been 'set aside' especially for colonisation, so as not to interfere with the rights exercised over the remaining, more valuable commons."[15]

At Mathon in the Eastern Region, in 1833, "a Hayward of the Common and wasteland was appointed in 1833, but his job was specifically 'to throw open abate and remove all incroachments now made or that shall hereafter be made upon the said Common or wastelands in the said Parish."[16]

In the Ross region, valued for high quality arable land, James Moir found "a marked concentration of the largest squatter settlements in the county" and on the hills on its southern boundary, geographically an extension of the Forest of Dean.

"The former commons in both Walford and Whitchurch parish had long been almost entirely overrun by squatter settlement; at Walford, for example, the Tithe Map recorded only 47 acres of common, 31 acres of which comprised the low-lying Coughton Marsh, the remaining acreage being scattered in a dozen small parcels, none of which exceeded four acres."[17]

When James Moir examined the Tithe returns for Herefordshire he found that "The Ross region commanded the highest value for both arable and pasture; it supported the largest squatter population, but had the lowest acreage of surviving commonland. In complete contrast, the neighbouring Black Mountains region was conspicuously badly off; it also had the largest surviving tracts of commonland, but the smallest number of "squatter settlements."

He describes how a visitor touring the Welsh Borderland area in 1814 saw the fragile huts of some would-be settlers and asked his travelling companion:

> "'These people are rent and tax free?'
> 'At present; perhaps they may not be so six months hence.'
> 'How say you? Surely the ground belongs to the public?'
> 'True it does; but I have known a team drove against such huts, for the purpose of pulling them down, when the builder could not pay 40s per annum,'"[19]

And he comments that the very fact that the visitor "specifies these huts as occupying only roadside verges and small parcels of waste implies that even heavier restrictions applied to the more valuable common pastures."

Obviously manorial lords would be least likely to tolerate encroachments on potentially profitable land, and Moir re-iterates that "agricultural improvement schemes were not the prime motive in applications for Enclosure Bills, but the desire to prevent further encroachments on the common."[20] He cites the case of four squatters from the Malvern Hills who were brought before the County Court in 1836 for riotous behaviour in resisting eviction. In court their council lamented the way

> "in which lords of the manor had come down upon poor persons and attempted to deprive them of their little property, with which were connected the most endearing recollections and upon which they had spent their labour..."[21]

He cites this case, not because it was representative of others, but because it is in fact the only example discovered of group resistance involving violence by squatters defending their 'rights' in the whole county and over the whole period 1780-1880. He finds little sign, in fact, of squatter communities "acting in unison, expressing their protests through popular forms of ritual or even overt acts of violence in the staunch defence of their rights."[22]

Given this situation, how did any of the Herefordshire squatter settlements survive and escape obliteration? Moir finds two main reasons. The first is that in so widely-squatted a county as Herefordshire,

"many of the owner-occupied settlements had effectively enclosed themselves, extinguishing all former common land by piecemeal encroachments and thus rendering any recourse to an Enclosure Award ratified by Parliament ineffectual, if not meaningless."[23]

His second reason is a reminder that a whole variety of individuals with different interests, whether as landlord, tenant, freeholder, labourer — or squatter, were affected by any Enclosure Award, and that while these awards have survived in large numbers, "the failure to reach an agreement may simply rest in an abortive meeting, for which no documentary evidence survives; or even in an unrecorded conversation in which the topic was aired but never pursued."[24]

Moir traces the tortuous history over 30 years of one particular attempt at Enclosure, that of the Doward and Llangrove Common between 1800 and 1833. At no point in the drama, he explains, did the squatters play any active role in the drama, yet they all eventually gained freehold. rights, independently of any Enclosure Act. "Can there be many comparable instances in history where such a large number of the labouring poor achieved so much by doing so little, while their numerous opponents, including all the most powerful members of the local community, did so much but achieved so little?"[25]

Several studies of squatter communities stress the sheer

variety of modes of getting a living that are characteristic of informal settlements. They are seen as pioneers of the industrial revolution. Barrie Trinder in Shropshire and Raphael Samuel exploring Headington Quarry, describe a great range of activities involving every member of the family. In the woods and fields of Herefordshire, James Moir asks, "If the typical commoner derived little benefit from the commons themselves, what was there in his modes of getting a living to distinguish him, if at all, from the ordinary villager or craftsman?" The only specialised

Headington Quarry, Oxfordshire in the early 20th century.
(PHOTO: RAPHAEL SAMUEL'S COLLECTION).

Raphael Samuel wrote *"These gardens were dug out of the waste, wherever there was an abandoned hollow or piece of waste. By the standards of the time — and even more of those today — they were quite unusually large, because land was freely available to those who asserted squatter's rights, gardens like this used to house a promiscuous variety of activities — laundry drying, poultry keeping, pig rearing as well as growing vegetables. Some are remembered as little orchards."*

industrial work Moir finds was among women on the Malvern Hills supplementing the household income with glove-stitching for the industry based in Worcester. But he follows through the seasons both the male and female cycles of work in the Herefordshire commons settlements.

Moir explores the links between the market centres and the squatter settlements. He explains how

"As transforming, modernising sectors within the broader framework of society, a certain correlation is again to be found between specialisation at the centre and squatter settlements at the periphery. Thus, cottages were perched on Wellington Heath on the outskirts of Ledbury, Bringsty Common and the Downs hosted sizeable settlements outside Bromyard, while similar clusters had mushroomed on Weobley Marsh (Weobley), Brick-kiln Common and Moseley Mere (Kington), Barewood (Pembridge), Peterstow, Upper Grove and Lower Grove Commons (Ross). The County Town itself was virtually encircled by commons settlements at Breinton, Eaton Bishop, Tillingham Common, Gorsty Common, Twyford Common, Dinedor Hill, Backbury Hill and Withington Marsh."[26]

The anthropologist Claude Levi-Strauss adopted the word *bricoleur* to describe the endless adaptability and capacity for improvisation and invention that characterise the builders of the squatter settlements that surround the cities of the southern hemisphere today. When James Moir explored the world of the typical Herefordshire squatters of the mid-nineteenth century, he found that this word, meaning roughly 'jack-of-all-trades' was, in all respects the best description for them.

References
1. William Plomer (ed) *Kilvert's Diary Volume Two, Aug 1871-May 1874*, London: Jonathan Cape 1939 p.224.
2. ibid *Vol One*, introduction. London: Jonathan Cape (1938) p.12.
3. *ibid Vol Two*, p.225.
4. J.W. Tonkin *Herefordshire*, London: B.T. Batsford 1977. p.70.
5. *ibid* p.77.
6. James Moir *'A World Unto Themselves'? Squatter Settlements in Herefordshire 1780-1880*, University of Leicester Ph.D. thesis 1990. (Unpublished).
7. *ibid* p.4.
8. *ibid* p.26.
9. *ibid* p.33.
10. cited in Ann R. Everton "Ty Un Nos" in *The Conveyancer and Property Lawyer* Vol XXXVI 1972 pp. 241-242.
11. James Moir *op cit*, citing local histories produced in 1955 and deposited in Herefordshire Record Office.
12. *ibid* citing 12th century histories, the *Islandingabok* and the *Landamabok*.
13. E.M. Leather *The Folklore of Herefordshire*, cited by Moir op cit p.163.
14. James Moir *op cit* p.165.
15. *ibid* p.45.
16. *ibid* p.51, citing the local Vestry Book.
17. *ibid* p.63.
18. *ibid* p.66.
19. *ibid* p.69, citing J.P. Malcolm *First Impressions*, 1814. p.102.
20. *ibid* p.287.
21. *ibid* p.271, citing *Herefordshire Journal* 13 January 1836.
22. *ibid* p.271.
23. *ibid* p.272.
24. *ibid* p.272.
25. *ibid* p.285.
26. *ibid* p.298

Chapter 9
Cradles of industry

"The open commons provided accommodation for workers in mines, ironworks and other major manufacturing concerns. They were also areas where consumer goods were made. The process of squatting on common land began in the sixteenth century. Sometimes squatters erected plots on the side of a common, sometimes on 'islands' in the middle. Often the lords of manors tacitly encouraged such settlement, particularly if labour was needed in the vicinity. Squatters could not be charged a rent for the use of common land, but they could be fined annually for encroachment. Their cottages were usually set in plots of about an acre, enclosed by a hedged earthen bank in which such useful plants as the damson, the hazel, the holly and rowan would be planted. Such settlements became the nuclei of large-scale industries in areas like the Black Country, the Forest of Dean and the Potteries. Others remained as service centres, providing goods and such services as well-digging or carting for the surrounding areas."

Barrie Trinder *The Making of the Industrial Landscape*[1]

The most-visited of all squatter cottages is the one lovingly re-erected by the Ironbridge Gorge Museum Trust at Coalbrookdale in Shropshire, in one of the five museums there celebrating the birthplace of the industrial revolution. It is at the Blists Hill Open Air Museum and children can buy a cut-and-fold cardboard model to build for themselves. The cottage was originally built between 1825 and 1841 at Burroughs Bank, Little Dawley, with walls of coal measure sandstone, a roof built of rough-hewn timber and

Squatter cottage from Burroughs Bank, Little Dawley: re-erected at Blists Hill Open Air Museum, Shropshire. (PHOTO: IRONBRIDGE GORGE MUSEUM TRUST).

(originally) a floor of beaten clay. In 1861 it was the home of Michael Corbett, a cobbler, his wife Sarah and their six children aged between 24 and 5 years old. On my first visit, Sylvia Bird was sitting at the table with the cat on her lap, making traditional shopping bags while explaining the history of squatters and inviting visitors to imagine how all the family could squeeze in. Barrie Trinder remarked that the cottage at Blists Hill is a "particularly crudely built" example, but of course it had to be, for didactic purposes. Usually in surviving houses of squatter origin there has been an evolution over time into a "normal" house, as extensive as that of any other home of the period.

Dr Trinder is an industrial archaeologist who was one of the pioneers of the Ironbridge Gorge Trust and encouraged generations of adult education students to explore the squatter cottages that mushroomed in the wake of the industrial revolution.[2] The chapter from one of his many books that I quote at the head of this account has the marvellously appropriate title "A landscape of Busy-Ness" And in his writings, the squatter settlements are no longer something on the margins of rural society, dominated by the great house and its upstairs-downstairs culture, landscaped gardens and docile cottagers. They become a peopled landscape where important things happened:

"Squatters made their living from a variety of sources. They cultivated their own plots and grazed their own beasts on the commons, but they could also exploit other resources there. In Cartmell commoners were able to take bracken, furze, and bound it into bundles for fuel. Above all, squatters were craftsmen. They became shoemakers, tailors or weavers. They dug pebbles from under the clay. They filled carts with sand and took it to building sites. They kept bees and sold the honey. Their wives baked cakes and acted as midwives. Such communities were of great importance in the establishment of major industries."[3]

With a group of his research students he instigated a long-term investigation of Holywell Lane, a squatter community of thirty or so cottages in Little Dawley, about a mile north east of Coalbrookdale. They were built between the early 16th and the mid 19th centuries by colliers and iron-workers, supplying the Darbys of Coalbrookdale where iron was first successfully smelted with coal in 1709. He remarked that 'open' industrial communities (as opposed to dwellings provided by entrepreneurs for their employees) "are rarely well-documented, and they often consist of ill-built dwellings which were easy targets for demolition by the public health officers of local authorities," The study of Holywell Lane, undertaken between 1972 and 1981 was just in time for one member of the group,

107

Maurice Hunt, to record the architecture for his dissertation and for another, Ken Jones, to interview the oldest local residents, and for John Malan as an archaeologist to excavate former cottage sites. It was found that

> "Some of the families fined in the 18th century for erecting cottages on the waste, the Evans, the Franks and the Gittins, were still living in the lane when the cottages were demolished in 1977. It appears that when one member of a family had encroached upon the waste to build a cottage, his relations would often build contiguous dwellings within the same plot... The reason for this remarkable continuity from one generation to another seems to be the nature of the holdings. Since the families concerned had built the cottages on the waste, it seems to have been assumed that one generation would succeed another even after they had been transferred to the rent roll. Such continuity is in contrast to the housing in the district built by entrepreneurs where there were always substantial changes in occupants from one census to another."[4]

Iron building materials, "made in profusion at nearby Coalbrookdale" were singularly absent from these cottages, and, as in so many self-built settlements, houses were enlarged to make space for additions to the family:

> "Many extensions resulted in odd-shaped rooms, low ceilings and door-heads, and awkward roof forms. The first floor rooms in one cottage would often extend over the ground floor rooms of its neighbour. Evidently neighbours must have been willing to share walls and to alter existing openings and roofs. The haphazard arrangements of rooms and the rough nature of the building work suggest that the cottagers laid out and built the dwellings themselves without skilled assistance."[5]

Similar home-made homes had sprung up in all those parts of Shropshire where iron ore and coal could be worked to feed the new blast furnaces. Trinder explains in another book how the cottages that had sprung up in Beveley and Coalpit Bank, which were encroachments on the wastes of the Leveson Gower estates in Shropshire "had all of the characteristics of squatter settlements, with houses of varying sizes built on plots of assorted shapes on what was once wasteland on the edges of Wombridge and Wellington parishes."[6] But two centuries of change have overlaid their original improvised character. The historian of the Welsh Borderlands, Dorothy Sylvester, explains the background to the identifiable settlements on the Clee Hills in terms of access to land:

"The increasing prosperity of the sixteenth and seventeenth centuries was associated with a rise in the population and a greater demand for land and houses, yet the growth of landed estates and the rise of ambitious yeoman farmers militated against the agrarian expansion of the rank and file. As a result, illegal enclosure or squatting became a feature of these centuries, and the tiny earthen and rough stone huts, and the small irregular enclosures around them combined, where land was scarce, to form a ragged edge to open commons as around the Clee Hills in south Shropshire where many remain to this day on Titterstone Clee, though on Brown Clee they have characteristically been engrossed into larger farms and estates."[7]

These marginal communities were on the fringes of both the pastoral peasant life and the birth of industry. Of the same area Barrie Trinder comments that

"Squatting on commons was a vitally important factor in the growth of the industrial West Midlands, but only in the Clee Hills in South Shropshire does there survive a landscape remotely like that of an eighteenth-century industrial squatting community. Ironworking ceased about 1840, coal mining declined and no town sprawled on to the hills. In consequence it is still possible to wander along packhorse tracks and among gorse and bracken on open commons, to pick over the spoil around bell pits and slag heaps and to see cottages in their hedged enclosures round the edges of commons and on islands in the middle."[8]

To the east, bounded by the River Severn, is the forest of Wyre, a hunting forest before the Norman conquest, which at that time was already being cleared and settled for farming. Victor Skipp explains how land-hungry peasants continued to form clearings or 'assarts' in the forest in the early Middle Ages:

"The population decline of the later Middle Ages doubtless brought a relaxation of pressure, but from the sixteenth to the nineteenth century many additional encroachments, legal and otherwise, led to a still further reduction in the size of the forest and to the development of relatively modern 'squatter' settlements such as Callow Hill and Far Forest."[9]

Still further to the east is the vast industrial conurbation of the Black Country, where innumerable part-time peasants combined stock-rearing with the blacksmith's trade, making not only spurs and bits and household ironmongery, but hand-welded chain and nail-making of every kind. As in Shropshire, there are few traces left today, beyond industrial dereliction, but Victor Skipp remarks that "Nevertheless, around the Gornals, in the street still called Rowley Village and at the little squatters' hamlet of Mushroom Green, it is not difficult to imagine those far-off days when each industry as there was took place in rural surroundings."[10]

The great landscape historian W.G. Hoskins cherished the nail-makers' red-brick cottages at Mushroom Green and linked them with the folklore of the one-night house, and with the contrasting enterprise of the big noble landowners:

"I think the little place called Mushroom Green must be a sardonic local joke for a place that grew up overnight. The squatters quickly put up their cottages; all over the Black Country people 'squatted' on the commons. If they could put up a house and get the smoke coming out of the chimney in twenty-four hours it was their freehold and the lord of the manor could not turn them off. The squatter believed in this immemorial right to put up his cottage overnight, but it also suited the lord of the manor who collected a small rent, and it provided a labour force for the industrial revolution which was just getting under way...

Mushroom Green was one of several squatters' settlements of nail-makers that sprang up almost overnight in the Black Country of Staffordshire.
(PHOTO: PETER JONES IN 1975).

"The landscape created by small men, by miner-farmers, a very small-scale landscape, was shaped at its other extreme by the influence of a noble family who owned about 25,000 acres on the edge of the Black Country. The Dudleys had immense mineral resources which they exploited — clay, coal, iron, limestone — everything they touched turned to money. You could say that the Black Country was robbed, and the Dudleys were the robber barons of the eighteenth and nineteenth centuries. While helping themselves to the minerals — which, of course, they owned — they took great care to exempt themselves by legislation from making any kind of compensation for things like mining subsidence, disturbance of surface pastures, and so on."[11]

Further north, in the upper Trent basin in Staffordshire is another great industrial conurbation — the Potteries. The five towns of Hanley, Burslem, Longton and Tunstall that coalesced to form Stoke-on-Trent must have had their squatter settlements of incomers and outworkers in the earthenware and china industries, long ago overtaken by new buildings which themselves have disappeared in the late 20th century. But subsidiary industrial activity sprang up in the villages on the fringe. Barry Trinder notes how "In the woodlands on the Staffordshire hills hearths were set up to make pliable the lengths of hazel used in the manufacture of the crates in which pottery was dispatched from North Staffordshire to the markets of the world."[12]

Another historian, Andrew Dobraszczyc, is famous for his social history walks in the Potteries, run by West Mercia Workers' Educational Association and his adult education classes from Keele University. One is his guided walk around Mow Cop, a mountainous ridge extending for three miles along the borders of Staffordshire and Cheshire, where in the early 19th century squatters, who were colliers, quarriers or sand carriers, built their originally thatched stone cottages in crofts enclosed piecemeal from the wasteland below the summit.

I joined another of his Sunday walks, around Baddeley Edge, also to the north of Stoke-on-Trent, armed with his pamphlet of map extracts and census figures from the 19th century, which was headed by an evocative contemporary description of the site by Henry Wedgwood:

"...Nor is the effect lessened by the rough stone-built cottages of Baddeley Edge as they snugly nestle themselves on the bosom of the hill, each cottage as you rise higher finding shelter under a steeper hill.

The hill is not so sterile as it looks for patches of well-cultivated ground occasionally meet the eye, and most of the cottages are belted with gardens that boast their fruit trees, which look beautiful from the hill, as you stand on the summit and look down the valley. But what adds greatly to the scene are the narrow sandy roads, fenced on both sides with stone walls and these intersect the hill in every form of curved lines, like network. Sometimes they wind, and twist, and cross each other in such a manner that the black stone walls, as they rise one above another, look like the ruins of some old pagan temple, hoary with age and time."[13]

Some of my fellow walkers had been to the session held on the previous day at Greenways Primary School, describing the colonisation of the wastes on the parish boundaries by squatters. Others were local residents, curious to learn the history of the gentrified houses of humble origins. We were all rewarded, for at every point Andrew Dobraszczyc brought to life the layers of the evolution of this haphazard landscape. We grasped how the precarious economy of quarrying, coal-mining, and then canal-boating had supported the families who settled strategically on the fringe of two parishes, to win a livelihood.

We almost felt we had met William Bailey, the collier who had rushed up a tiny stone house with its vegetable garden, and then had his annual fine for encroachment turned into a rent, and in time became a freeholder. Once taught how to look we could recognise the stages by which his house had grown. And indeed, one of the neighbours came out to tell us about his successor Joe Evans, who had died only a few years earlier and was remembered because he had planted the evergreen hedge around the Ebenezer Baptist Chapel opposite. Thanks to the diligent explorers of "history on the ground" the squatters of the industrial revolution were closer to us than we had imagined.

References
1. Barrie Trinder *The Making of the Industrial Landscape,* (1982) Gloucester: Alan Sutton 1987 p.40.
2. B. Trinder "Industrial Rookeries in Shropshire". Report of paper from *Industrial Communities. The Proceedings of a Symposium on Industrial Colonies, Settlements and Planned Communities* held at the University of Aston in October 1974.
3. Barrie Trinder *The Making...* p.48.
4. Ken Jones, Maurice Hunt, John Malam and Barrie Trinder "Holywell Lane: A Squatter Community in the Shropshire Coalfield" *Industrial Archaeology Review* Vol VI No 3, Autumn 1982 pp. 163-185. Off-print published by Ironbridge Gorge Museum p.73.
5. *ibid* p.171.
6. Barrie Trinder *The Industrial Revolution in Shropshire,* Chichester: Phillimore 1973 p.321.
7. Dorothy Sylvester *The Rural Landscape of the Welsh Borderlands: a study in historical geography,* London: Macmillan 1969 p.134.
8. Barrie Trinder *The Making...* p.253.
9. Victor Skipp *The Centre of England,* London: Eyre Methuen 1979 p.52.
10. *ibid* p.203.
11. W.G. Hoskins *One Man's England,* London: BBC 1978 p.53.
12. Barrie Trinder *The Making...* p.84.
13. Henry Wedgwood *Romance of Staffordshire,* c. 1878, quoted in Andrew Dobraszczyc *A walk around Baddeley Edge,* Stoke-on-Trent: West Mercia WEA Social History Walks 1993 p.1.

Chapter 10
At the rough end of Oxford

"Old men could remember when the Rise, covered with juniper bushes, stood in the midst of a furzy heath — common land, which had come under the plough after the passing of the Enclosure Acts. Some of the ancients still occupied cottages on land which had been ceded to their fathers as "squatters rights", and probably all the small plots upon which the houses stood had originally been so ceded. In the eighteen-eighties the hamlet consisted of about thirty cottages and an inn, not built in rows, but dotted down anywhere within a more or less circular group. A deeply rutted cart track surrounding the whole, and separate houses or groups of houses were connected by a network of pathways..."

Flora Thompson *Lark Rise to Candleford*[1]

Flora Thompson was born in 1876, and the Lark Rise of her book was the hamlet of Juniper Hill, three miles from Brackley in Oxfordshire. Her biographer explains that the old couple known in her book as Dick and Sally, in their old cottage with a large garden, were Richard and Sarah Moss, who used to ask the young Flora to write their letters for them, as she was thought to be something of a scholar:

"Sarah Moss was one of the few hamlet people old enough to remember when heathland had surrounded the houses. Born in 1812, Sarah was a last link between the world of the dispossessed labourer and that of her own father who had commoners' rights, keeping a cow, geese, poultry and pigs on the common and owning a donkey cart to carry his pro-

115

duce to the market. Enclosure of common land was the first step, in the process which turned the independent English peasant farmer into the twentieth-century proletariat."[2]

A few miles to the north-east of Oxford there is a round fen called Otmoor, surrounded by a ring of hamlets, known as the "seven towns" whose cottagers kept large numbers of geese on the common. A long series of attempts at parliamentary enclosure by landlords like the Duke of Marlborough and Lord Abingdon were made from 1801 onwards and were finally enforced. Fences were erected, and Lord Churchill's troop of Yeomanry Cavalry were sent to protect them.

But, explain J.L. and Barbara Hammond,

"the inhabitants were not overawed. They determined to perambulate the bounds of Otmoor in full force, in accordance with the old custom. On Monday, 6th September (1830) five hundred men, women and children assembled from the Otmoor towns and they were joined by five hundred more from elsewhere. Armed with reap-hooks, hatchets, bill-hooks and duckets, they marched in order round the seven-mile-long boundary of Otmoor, destroying all the fences on their way. By noon their work of destruction was finished."[3]

It was, of course, in vain, though when Paul Barker went to Otmoor in 1998 he was told that it was the struggle against enclosure there that gave rise to the well-known verse

The fault is great in Man or Woman
Who steals the Goose from off a Common;
But who can plead that man's excuse
Who steals the Common from the Goose?[4]

Many other Oxford villages have their squatter folklore. Wootton, near Woodstock has a reputed one-night house, and the history of a pair of cottages at Wolvercote, now part of the city itself, which were demolished about 1930, was unravelled by John Rhodes and his colleagues from the Oxfordshire Museum Service, starting with a photograph from the 1880s. They were probably built early in the 19th century by squatters on a patch of land by the Toll Bridge.

> "By the end of the century the two cottages had been knocked into one, and were lived in by the Long family. Mother and father, helped by two daughters, made 'pimps' for the Oxford colleges: wire-tied bundles of firewood. Two sons worked at the nearby Paper Mill, and another on the railway as an 'engineer.' Behind the cottages, on a small creek, was a boathouse where at least one son slept."[5]

Such accounts evoke the "landscape of busy-ness" described by Barrie Trinder in his account of the making of the industrial landscape, as firstly canals and river navigations and then the railways revolutionised transport.[6] And from Oxford came a marvellously detailed oral history of life and labour in a squatter community.[7] For many years I made an annual visit to Oxford Brookes University (formerly much loved as Oxford Polytechnic) to talk to members of the course at CENDEP, which stands for the Centre for Development and Emergency Planning, at the invitation of Nabeel Hamdi, the author of *Housing Without Houses*.[8] I had more to gain from course members than to give them, since they came from Africa, Latin America, the Indian subcontinent and South-East Asia with, absorbing experiences of the problems and opportunities of the unofficial self-built and squatter settlements that surround every city in those continents.

117

However, my task there was usually to give an account of the lessons to be gained from a hundred years of public housing policy in Britain. It was a dispiriting job, because course members found it hard to get used to the idea of a country where both official regulation and control of land are so buttoned-up and inescapable that poor people can do nothing to house themselves but accept the official solutions, rejected by anyone with any freedom of choice. The course members found it hard to understand the mind-set of a rich country where, as Simon Fairlie put it, "It is the planning system, rather than ownership, that is now the main way in which ordinary people are prevented from 'reclaiming the land.'"[9]

The actual postal address of Oxford Brookes University is Gipsy Lane, Headington, indicating that the site was once a gipsy encampment and that only a mile up the road was Headington Quarry, one of the few squatter settlements in Britain whose history has been carefully retrieved before the place disappeared in the usual suburban expansion of the city. This was thanks to the work of Raphael Samuel, most of whose working life was spent as a tutor at Ruskin College (not part of the University) at Oxford, where he instigated the first annual History Workshop in 1967. At the second History Workshop he read a paper on "proletarian Oxfordshire" and in the next few years he was in time to record the recollections of very old local people, and to use this evidence together with manuscript and printed sources, since it often enabled the historian, "even from comparatively few pieces of written evidence... to make some quite substantial sense."[10] He showed this, marvellously, in his essay "'Quarry roughs': life and labour in Headington Quarry 1860-1920".[11]

With a beautifully recorded English squatter settlement almost on the doorstep, Nabeel Hamdi suggested that I should outline the story of Headington Quarry to course members and conclude with a walk-around on the site. So I spent a day plodding the neat streets, punctuated by primary schools and play spaces, to seek out survivals from the past. I found that the various old stone quarries had been filled or levelled, or encompassed by sites like the Quarry Fields Recreation Ground, and that family names I had picked up from Raphael Samuel's account are perpetuated in the new street names.

There were too few visible survivals from the past to justify my taking up the time of course members on a visit, so they had to be content with a classroom exposition. On that particular year, however, we were joined by Raphael Samuel, who, though seriously ill, happened to be at Ruskin College that day. He died later that year. He stressed that in some senses, the history of apparently marginal settlements like the Quarry was more characteristic of the rural past than our usual assumptions supposed, and that ancient folkways survived there. This point was verified for me by one of those Quarry street names: William Kimber Crescent.

Among the inconsequential memories we all have from childhood, I can vividly remember, in the late 1930s, poring over the very small section of the Columbia record catalogue devoted to folk music. It was dominated by the 78rpm discs of Will Kimber playing his concertina. The BBC Sound Archive has a recording of Kimber explaining that at Christmas 1899, because the weather was too bad for any work in the building trades, he and the Quarry morris men, to earn a few pence, performed outside Sandfield Cottage, Old Headington. A visitor asked him to come back and play a couple of tunes again. Kimber obliged and was astonished when his new admirer played both of them back to him on the piano. He was rewarded with a glass of wine and half a sovereign from his new friend: Cecil Sharp.[12] Raphael Samuel put the incident in context:

> "It is perhaps this self-sufficiency which explains —
> or helps to explain Quarry's survival as a morris-
> dancing village, certainly the feature for which it is
> best known, for it was here, in 1899, that the

English morris was rediscovered by Cecil Sharp. When Quarry people went dancing it was to the tunes of a local fiddler or accordionist — many of them, it seems, learnt from the local gypsy who 'had lots of old tunes' (the leading fiddler of the 1870s, Sampson Smith, was a local gypsy, and he also danced on the local morris side.) Quarry was a very musical village, but the music was its own: there were no brass bands."[13]

The exploration of the Quarry had grown out of a project that Raphael Samuel had set for his first year students in investigating disputes over common land at Headington, known as the Open Magdalens and the Open Brasenose. There had been questions for which documents in the County Record Office provided no answers, but where an oral history approach might add understanding. The exercise revealed more than was anticipated: a whole community of squatter origin that provided the building materials for 19th century Oxford, and which took in its washing. Most of the expanding cities and towns of Victorian Britain had such service settlements beyond their fringes. In London there was Notting Dale "settled by some refugee pig-keepers from Marble Arch to be joined later by gypsies and brick-makers." It became the laundry for Notting Hill and Kensington, just as Kensal New Town ('Soapsuds Island') served the fashionable districts of Bayswater and Belgravia as "a chief recipient for the weekly washings of the rich."

The entire land surface of the village had been quarried for stone for the building of the Oxford colleges over five centuries and in the 19th century, clay-pits were added for brick-making. Raphael Samuel learned that the earliest dwellings were "poor insubstantial hovels which could without difficulty be removed and set up elsewhere" and old residents told him how the village was studded with ownerless spots of land "nobody's land", "useless land" — "where the enterprising opportunist could put up a cottage, or extend a garden, more or less at will."[15]

The equivocal legal status of the land, together with stone and clay and the skills to meet the city's demands, led to housebuilding and the sharing within the village of constructional abilities. At the same time it enabled a varied series of poaching, rabbit-snaring, pig-rearing and cow-keeping activities. Every family had a garden or allotment and used a remarkable series of gathering techniques to exchange within the community, or to sell to the farmers or to the city. Samuel records that the importance of the vast variety of activities of Quarry families was that, however poor, they stayed alive outside the official system of poor relief. Neither in the official census returns nor in the recollections he gathered from old villagers "in all the hardships they speak about" is any mention made "of those two great standbys of the out-of-work elsewhere: the workhouse and parish relief." He tells us that,

"The notion of common rights was built in to the cottager's economy, and so too was that of personal independence: it was possible to make 'a bit of a living' even when wage-paid labour gave out, and even when there was no money, to keep the table supplied with food, and have enough fuel to feed the fire. Perhaps it is this which helps to explain why Quarry, though 'rough' by the standards of more regulated communities, seems to have escaped the kind of destitution so familiar in the late Victorian countryside and so rampant in the towns. Subsistence never gave out, however severe the season, nor was charity ever called upon to take its place — there was little available save that which the working population of the village provided for themselves."

In the context of the history of the English poor, steering

121

clear of the hated and feared Poor Law provision was a remarkable achievement, and Headington Quarry was also, as Raphael Samuel noted, a village which had arisen singularly free of landlords. "For centuries it had enjoyed what was virtually an extra-parochial existence, a kind of anarchy, in which the villagers were responsible to nobody but themselves."

Indeed, for any student of the informal economy in the squatter settlements of the southern hemisphere today, any of the relationships and connections between the official, recognised, GNP-included economy and the unofficial sector that actually keeps people alive, the story of Headington Quarry is fascinating. The village was outside the stereotyped economy of wage labour and capital. Samuel notes how

> "Numbers of villagers escaped the servitudes of wage labour altogether, and there were many more for whom employment was characteristically short term and indirect. Within the village nothing like a capitalist class emerged. In building, the smaller jobs were often taken on by a pair of mates, or by individuals acting on their own, or with a helper. Stone-digging work and navvying were often in the hands of 'companionships' — self-selecting bands of men, linked to one another by ties of friendship or blood and sometimes both."

Within the sexual division of labour "women's work" was, overwhelmingly, washing clothes and linen for the colleges, chapels and affluent houses of Oxford, and this of course engendered a sub-trade for delivery boys, carriers' carts and even laundry-basket making. In the "male trades", stone had been quarried there for centuries, so there were both quarrymen and masons, as well as all the humbler work associated with stone, from producing cobbles for street paving to gathering the rubble from which houses in and out of Quarry were built. But the local geology also provided clay for brickmaking, which remained a family activity. Samuel notes that "No dynasty of brick-makers appeared, even in the heyday of the industry's local prosperity, nor was there a decisive separation of wage labour and capital." In the whole range of the build-ing trades, there was a bias towards "rough, open-air work." At the same time it was a rural place, so there was subsistence small-holding, horticulture, and the whole world of allotment-gardening, pig-keeping, poultry-rear-ing, poaching, and gleaning fuel and much else, from the woods. Apart from the busy exchange of goods and service within the village, everything had a market, from rabbits to leaf-mould, holly berries and moss, sold to the florist's shops of the city.

By comparison with landless labourers in other parishes, the squatters of Headington Quarry had won a degree of independence which was tenaciously enlarged over time. Samuel cited the complaint of the churchwar-dens about the Steel and Parsons families there. "Some forty or fifty years ago two small huts were erected upon this land, and they were inhabited by some poor people, and from time to time the buildings have increased into two cottages and the occupants have enclosed a piece of the ground as gardens, but for none of this did they pay any rent."

After the first world war, the coming of motor-buses ended the separateness of the Quarry, and made avail-able jobs in the growing motor industry at Cowley. The building of new properly-surfaced roads made a link with Old Headington and beyond. The acquisition of land by speculative builders and the eventual incorpora-tion of the village into the Oxford city boundaries in 1936 brought an end to the squatter village which had been completely redeveloped by the post-war decades. Its origins would have been forgotten but for the documen-tary exploration and the 'just in time' interviews with survivors made by Raphael Samuel and his students in the late 1960s.

References

1. Flora Thompson *Lark Rise to Candleford* (1939) Harmondsworth: Penguin Books 1973. p.17.
2. Gillian Lindsay *Flora Thompson: the story of the Lark Rise writer*, London: Robert Hale 1990 pp. 25-6.
3. J.L. and Barbara Hammond *The Village Labourer Vol I*, (1911) London: Guild Books 1948. pp. 83-92.
4. Paul Barker "The looking-glass world of Otmoor" *New Statesman* June 1998. p.54.
5. Crispin Paine and John Rhodes (eds) *The Worker's Home: small houses in Oxfordshire through three centuries*, Woodstock: Oxfordshire Museum Service 1979.
6. Barrie Trinder *The Making of the Industrial Landscape*, (1982) Gloucester: Alan Sutton 1982. pp. 12-51.
7. Raphael Samuel "'Quarry roughs': life and labour in Headington Quarry 1860-1920" in R. Samuel (ed.) *Village Life and Labour*, London: Routledge and Kegan Paul 1975.
8. Nabeel Hamdi *Housing Without Houses: participation, flexibility, enablement*, New York: Van Nostrand. 1991, London: Intermediate Technology Publications 1995.
9. Simon Fairlie *Low Impact Development: planning and people in a sustainable countryside*, Oxford: Jon Carpenter 1996.
10. Raphael Samuel "Headington Quarry: Recording a Labouring Community" in "The Interview in Social History", Part One of the report of a conference held by the Social Science Research Council at the University of Leicester on March 23rd to March 25th 1972. *Oral History* Vol I No 4, 1972. p.122.
11. Raphael Samuel "'Quarry roughs'" *op cit* p.156.
12. William Kimber in a recorded interview (n.d.) in the BBC Sound Archive, includes in "The Folk Revival in Britain", Programme 1, BBC Radio 2, 25 August 1999.
13. Raphael Samuel "'Quarry roughs'" *op cit* p.162.
14. *ibid* p.142.
15. *ibid* p.142.

Chapter 11
Roadside settlements

"In Ancient Countryside a characteristic feature is the sudden narrowing of the highway where a cottage in a long narrow garden has been built on it. Some formerly wide main roads — e.g. north and south of Braintree, or between Birmingham and Stratford-on-Avon or south of Sherbourne (Dorset) have such 'squatter' houses and gardens, which may themselves be of some antiquity, going on one after another for miles within the original width of the road."

Oliver Rackham *The History of the Countryside*[1]

Many of us, when travelling by road, notice cottages at the very roadside and reflect that the people who built so close to the traffic were lacking in foresight. We fail to reflect on the sheer emptiness of the road for most of its history, and until the avalanche of motor traffic in the mid-20th century. But cottages of that long and narrow roadside kind were the most characteristic form of squatter housing, taking the form of *purprestures* or encroachments, which from the 12th century onward took up much of the time of manorial courts. Oliver Rackham gives half a dozen examples and explains how purprestures could occur on any common land, but "Most often took the form of narrowing a road, either by a neighbouring farmer pushing out his frontage or by a third party setting up a smallholding within the road itself. Manorial courts often condoned purprestures on payment of an annual fine to the lord of the manor."[2] But roads themselves, because of ruts, sloughs and muddy pitfalls, as Rackham puts it, had grown ever wider.

This was true especially of the ancient drift or drove roads, trodden by herds of cattle and sheep, but it also applied to local lanes before and after the Enclosures. The historian of country lanes explains how,

"The effect of enclosure of the lanes was that wherever it took place the existing pattern of routes was replaced with a new and generally much simpler one. The new roads were built straight where possible, and to allow for by-passing of the sloughs which developed along them in winter they were made immensely wide: inter village roads were 12 metres in width, roads between market towns were 18 metres, and the main road to London through Rutland was no less than 30 metres across. Much of this breadth became grass verge, especially after Macadam's innovation had arrived to dispose of the sloughs..."[3]

The kind of cottage that "rose like a lark from the furrows" on roadside wastes can be seen in many parts of England — in Essex villages, for example at Great Horkesley on the Colchester to Sudbury road, and in north Bedfordshire in the hamlets of Eaton Socon, Colnworth, Keysoe and Roxton. At Airton in North Yorkshire, on the green at the junction with the old market road from Settle to Ripon, is a house known as the squatter's house, surrounded by a walled garden. Inevitably, the guidebook explains that "this is a reminder of the times when anyone could lay a claim to land on which he managed, during a 24-hour period, to construct a dwelling and have smoke coming out of the chimney — or perhaps in those days a hole in the roof."[4]

The historian of village greens, Brian Bailey, noticed how at Morton Pinkney in Northamptonshire, among other places, "the winding road through the village wove its way between squatters' cottages on the original green leaving little more than wide grass verges."[5] And a friend

A 17th century squatter cottage on the green at Airton, Yorkshire.
(PHOTO: LEE WRIGHT).

who is always alert to the unofficial environment, Brian
Richardson, described his experience:

> "What I noticed when motorcycling through
> Gloucestershire, Worcestershire and Herefordshire
> (particularly along the A417 road which is rich in
> examples) was that a typical characteristic was that
> such a house was long and narrow in plan, parallel
> with the highway and very close to it, and tall, so as
> to get the most on its footprint. Not only is there lit-
> tle or no front garden, but a very shallow back gar-
> den too — sometimes one can see through the house
> from front to back, the rear hedge close to the far
> window. And the garden is long, with cultivation at
> the end(s) of the house, and tapering, so that the
> intrusion into the highway land is imperceptible.
> Once you see one you see lots!"[6]

He also tells me of a 'double' squat, one house in front of another, also on the A417 between Sledge Green and Long Green, near Tewkesbury, adding that "On this road, at the boundary of Hereford and Worcester in Hollybush, is a common on the lower slope of the Malverns that is peppered with tiny cottages at random intervals like fallen leaves blown by the wind." On the other side of the hills at Malvern Chase, the historian of Hanley Castle notes a survey of enclosed land in 1721 with "unflattering references to the 'pilfering hoard' who seemed to camp out in shacks on the common land near the estates of the more socially acceptable."[7]

In the early years of the 20th century, the drift from the land, in the form of the depopulation of rural England, was seen as a social disaster, needing remedies. The appalling state of housing for the 'labouring classes' was one of the explanations given. Whether the cold, sodden and insanitary homes of Edwardian rural society were 'tied' cottages, provided for employees by farmers, or whether they were rented from village landlords, they were notorious. Many observers felt that some of the worst were owner-occupied homes, built by the poor for the poor. There was a vast literature on this theme, ranging from the reports commissioned by the government at the turn of the century from the novelist Rider Haggard[8] to J.W. Robertson Scott's *England's Green and Pleasant Land* of 1925, still considered relevant when reprinted after the second world war, which described the sheer horror of the housing of rural workers.[9]

One of the housing reformers was Dr William Savage, Medical Officer of Health for Somerset, whose account of rural housing was published in 1915, when powerful people had other preoccupations. He provided photographs of the front and rear elevations of houses built on wasteland by the roadside in his county, and his caption read,

"They abut on one side on the road, and on the other upon fields, and have no gardens back or

The front and back of houses built on wasteland by the roadside in Somerset.
(PHOTO: W.J. READ – EARLY 20TH CENTURY).
From William G. Savage: Rural Housing, 1915.

front. Most of the houses are owned by the occupiers. The houses are of the poorest description and are full of sanitary defects. When photographed they had been improved to some extent, chiefly by making the windows to open and by the provision of rain gutters and down-shuting (rain-water pipes) in front. There is no space for sanitary conveniences, but wedged between the houses, usually in sheds, are what used to be offensive privies, and are now pail closets. There is no land available to empty the contents. The water supply is from contaminated shallow wells, this block having two, also between the houses. Steps have been under consideration for the past four or five years to obtain a pure piped supply."[10]

These home-made homes were neither better nor worse than the houses provided by farmers for their employees, condemned and demolished in large numbers in the inter-war and post-war years as unfit for human habitation, only to be rediscovered as precious relics of vernacular architecture.

The engineer L.C.T. Holt was a campaigner for the revival of inland waterways and for saving the integrity of the railway network, and left behind several volumes of autobiography, in the last of which he described the changes in the West Country village where his family lived:

"Because of misapplication of the well-intentioned Slum Clearance Acts by a zealous Medical Officer of Health, most of the old village cottages I knew were condemned on grounds of their low ceilings or lack of through-ventilation. Even with the aid of the available local authority grants, their occupants could not afford alterations which would conform with local regulations. Consequently, such houses have been acquired by those who could afford reconstruction, executives or retired business men, with the result that they have been 'prettified' beyond recognition and embellished with such things as bogus wrought iron work of welded steel strip, carriage lanterns or wooden wheelbarrows filled with flowers. Meanwhile such old village families as have survived this upheaval live in council houses on the village outskirts, from whence they are collected and delivered daily by special coaches which take them to work in the nearby factories."[11]

By the early years of another century, the new council houses, with all those modest facilities that had been beyond their reach for years, have been sold in the private market, and the factories on the fringe of the nearest town have closed because of the logic of the market.

The mere mention of the history of inland waterways and railways as alternatives to roads is a reminder that they too developed new forms of unofficial settlements. These were the temporary settlements of the men known as navvies, who dug and tunnelled, with a shockingly high casualty and mortality rate. Many of their shanty-towns evolved into permanent hamlets or extensions to existing towns and villages to meet the needs of people in search of an income. Their history is being garnered by the industrial archaeologists, and I should mention just a few of those shifting the boundaries between recognised and unofficial, unacknowledged settlements. W.G. Hoskins wrote about "the fascinating canal settlement of Shardlow (in Derbyshire) on the Trent and Mersey Canal"[12] and the historians of the railway builders describe how they were housed "in any of four ways: private lodges, sod huts, shants, properly regulated settlements."[13]

John Rhodes, Director of Museums in Gloucester, told me how in that city, a group of shanties was situated beside the ship canal, "and so may have originated as a navvy settlement, but it outlived the completion of the canal in 1827. On being evicted from High Orchard in the late 1830s the shanty dwellers moved to California and Newtown, where their tiny huts were plotted by the Ordnance Survey in 1883 shortly before demolition. The census returns of 1841 and 1851 show a large part of the Gloucester population living as lodgers in desperate over-crowding which the shanty settlements will have allevi-ated."[14] Terry Coleman, in his account of *The Railway Navvies*, describes the way their shacks and shanty settle-ments varied in their degree of civilisation:

> "On the South Devon Railway at Totnes in the mid-dle forties the huts were made of mud and turf. The most usual way of throwing them up was to burrow a short way into a bank, so that the back and part of the sides of the hut would be formed by solid earth, and then make a roof of spare rafters and timbers."[15]

On the other hand, "To this day, near Four Marks in Hampshire, a large wooden building stands by the side of the A31, only a hundred yards or so from the London to Southampton line. It is now a pub, and its sign-board bears the name of 'The Shant'."[16]

The roadside was, of course, the traditional site of gypsy encampments and that of people forced into migrancy by disaster or misfortune. Defoe in his *Journal of the Plague Year* describes how a party of refugees from the plague in London in 1665, found an old decayed roadside cottage and went to work to make it weathertight:

> "and in a very few Days made it capable to shelter them all in case of bad weather, and in which there was an old Chimney, and an old Oven, tho' both lying in Ruins, yet they made them both fit for Use, and raising Additions, Sheds, and Leantoo's on every side they soon made the House capable to hold them all."[17]

At the end of the 19th century, British roads were, offi-cially, more free of traffic than at any time for centuries.

The elaborate network of stage coaches had been replaced by comfortable and efficient railway transport. With an incredible network of branch lines, bringing a series of new technologies to rural life, a glimpse of the outside world previously taken for granted by their social superiors, was offered to the poor. At the same time agriculture was in a deep depression, with farm bankruptcies every week. What happened on the verges of the neglected country roads was insignificant, while planning controls were half a century ahead. Roadside shanties were the business of few, apart from local constables and absentee landlords, spending their inheritance elsewhere. The memories of people who were young in the early years of the 2oth century include recollections of residents in improvised but long-term shelters, often seen as preferred alternatives to the workhouse. I came by chance upon this touching news report of 1921 from Herefordshire:

"William Mayo (73), who lived in a wretched hovel beside the common at Woolhope and who earned a precarious living by selling firewood, besoms and skewers, had been a cripple from birth. Having hardly any power in the legs, he used to drive in a dilapidated cart, drawn by a donkey. On Tuesday, after a stay in Ledbury workhouse, he started to drive for 'home'. The weather was wild and, as he suffered from bronchitis, he decided to sleep for two nights in the outhouses of inns. At length, without food, he reached his hovel, one end of which had been blown down by the gale a few nights before.

"His wife (whom he had married when he was 65) made a fire outside the hovel and sat with him all night. In the morning she went to make him some tea and when she returned she found him dead. The workhouse doctor was not at the inquest, but had told a policeman that death was due to exposure on the common and natural causes."[18]

Of course the characteristic, seasonal roadside settlers have, for hundreds of years, been the the Gypsies. Their historian, Sir Angus Fraser concludes that their main achievement, while managing to preserve a distinct identity and while "clinging tenaciously to some ideal of community and independence and self-employment" has been to survive at all. The last time when anyone was hanged in England for being a wandering Gypsy was in the 1650s when at Bury St Edmunds in Suffolk 13 people were executed for this crime. The Vagrancy Act of 1822 declared that "all persons pretending to be Gypsies", telling fortunes, wandering abroad or lodging in tents, carts or wagons were to be deemed rogues and vagabonds with a penalty of up to six months' imprisonment.[19]

Like the Irish tinkers and Scottish travellers, the wandering people provided essential services in rural Britain, from tin-smithery to harvest labour. It wasn't their fault that the Enclosures took away most wasteland, and that the industrialisation of farming eliminated much seasonal employment, now restricted to part-time local gangs of unemployed people, juveniles and the 'black' economy. Travelling people have adapted to such modern equivalents as tarmac-laying and car-breaking. But in the decades following the second world war the situation of Gypsies was made progressively worse, with terrible scenes (and some actual deaths) in dawn battles in the 1960s between travelling people and bailiffs employed by local councils and backed by the police.[20]

The Caravan Sites Act of 1968 required local authorities to provide sites for Gypsies and other travellers, with a one hundred per cent grant from central government to defray the cost. In 1992 Sir George Young, Minister of State for Housing and Planning, announced his intention of ending the obligation on councils to provide sites, and proposed to make it a criminal rather than a civil offence to park a caravan on any land without the landowners' consent, and to enable local authorities to confiscate vehicles. He said that the Act of 1968 had failed, since only 38 per cent of councils had complied with it.[21]

Five years earlier, the government had asked Gerald Wibberley, a much-respected emeritus Professor of Countryside Planning, to report on the workings of the Act. He had concluded that "The Act is working, slowly, but quite well in a few areas, even though councils and government didn't have their hearts in it." He added that, in the light of his report, "It is sad to me that the government have allowed themselves to take an ethnic cleansing approach."[22]

In introducing the new legislation, Sir George Young had declared that it was the responsibility of travellers to acquire their own land for sites and to apply for planning consent. A number have done so, and almost invariably planning permission has been refused.[23] The most recent form of roadside dwellers are those known as New Age Travellers or the Convoy. Every year a caravan of wanderers in old buses or caravans converge in the vicinity of Stonehenge and infuriates residents, the police and newspaper readers. Tim Mars reported their interview responses to me:

"Several members interviewed contrasted the convoy way of life explicitly with living in the cities, and described it as a consciously chosen alternative. They feared that the current harassment and impounding of vehicles is likely to leave them with no choice but to go back to the cities. They talked about a difference in quality of life between being unemployed in the city and unemployed in the community of the convoy. They talked about their right to choose the convoy way of life and not to be forced to live in the city. In choosing mobile accommodation, the convoyers are effectively exploiting the only remaining loophole (thanks to the traditional rights of bone fide gypsies and holiday caravanners) available to people without cash, mortgage credit-

worthiness or access to New Town rented accommodation who nevertheless are determined to escape
the city — a loophole which, as we can see, is currently being mercilessly tightened."[24]

References

1. Oliver Rackham *The History of the Countryside*, London: J.M. Dent 1986, p.278.
2. *ibid* p.265.
3. Gareth Lovatt Jones *English Country Lanes*, London: Wildwood House 1988, p.163.
4. R. and M. Freethy *Discovering the Yorkshire Dales*, Edinburgh: John Donald Ltd 1991, pp. 54-5.
5. Brian Bailey *The English Village Green*, London: Robert Hale 1985, p.30.
6. Brian Richardson, personal communication, 17 Oct 1998.
7. Pamela Hurle *Hanley Castle: heart of Malvern Chase*, Chichester: Phillimore 1978, pp. 124-5.
8. H. Rider Haggard *Rural England.*
9. J.W. Robertson Scott *England's Green and Pleasant Land*, (1925), Harmondsworth: Penguin Books 1947.
10. William G. Savage *Rural Housing*, London: T Fisher Unwin 1915, pp.55-6.
11. L.C.T. Holt *Landscape with Figures*, Gloucester: Alan Sutton 1992, p.88.
12. W.G. Hoskins *Fieldwork in Local History*, (1967), London: Faber 1982, p.11.
13. Dick Sullivan *Navvyman*, London: Coracle Books 1983, p.73.
14. John Rhodes, personal communication, 1 October 1992, citing Gloucestershire,: *The Victoria County History* Vol IV pp. 223, 225, 228.
15. Terry Coleman *The Railway Navvies* (1965), Harmondsworth: Penguin 1968, p.82.
16 *ibid* p.83
17. Daniel Defoe *A Journal of the Plague Year*, (1722) London: George Routledge 1896, p.193.
18. Report in *Daily Herald* 24 January 1921.
19. Angus Fraser *The Gypsies*, Oxford: Basil Blackwell 1993
20. Derek Hawes and Barbara Perez *The Gypsy and the State: the ethnic cleansing of British society* (2nd ed), Bristol: Policy Press 1996, p.23.
21. *The Guardian* 19 August 1992.

22. Gerald Wibberley on BBC *Look East* 22 November 1992.
23. Donald Kenrick and Colin Clark *Moving On: the gypsies and travellers of Britain*, Hatfield: University of Hertfordshire Press 1999.
24. Tim Mars, reported in *Welcome, Thinner City*, London: Bedford Square Press 1989.

Chapter 12
On the far side of enclosure

"As the concept of absolute ownership emerged in the post medieval period, landlords increasingly came to think of the commons as 'their' property. They regarded ancient customs and common rights as part of a rather old-fashioned tenurial system, which was also essentially subversive, and a dangerous threat to the discipline of the labour force. Common lands provided poor cottagers with a certain amount of independence. They could gain a portion of their subsistence through exploiting the wastes, and were therefore discouraged from entering full-time employment as labourers. To many landlords this limited independence seemed far from desirable,"

Tom Williamson & Liz Bellamy *Property and Landscape.*[1]

There are several English villages, like Soham in Cambridgeshire and Braunton in Devon, where strip cultivation in open fields survives, but only at Laxton in Nottinghamshire do the three fields and the village democracy of a 12-man jury with a foreman for each field and a bailiff still exist. Their significance was first stressed by Gilbert Slater in his study from 1907 of *The English Peasantry and the Enclosure of Common Fields*, and was carefully interpreted in the 1930s by C.S. and C.S. Orwin in their book, now regarded as a classic, on *The Open Fields*. When it first appeared it was reviewed with enthusiasm by Herbert Read, a farmer's son who concluded that:

"It is not claimed that the open fields system was ideal; poverty and hardship existed, and in the background was the feudal system, exacting service rents, payments in kind, tithes, etc. But at any rate the system demonstrates two facts so often denied: that a democracy does not necessarily imply a State or a bureaucracy; and that an industry can be administered by the workers themselves, without capital and without overseers. In short, the history of the open fields is a proof of the main principles of anarchism."[2]

This opinion, now over sixty years old, illustrates the variety of possible views that can be held on the facts of enclosure. Most of us tend to retain the version passed on to us at school. When I was a primary school pupil in the early 1930s, the history texts handed out in class once a week were the Piers Plowman Junior Histories, the progressive and well-illustrated school texts of the inter-war years. Consulting the copies in the archive of the Institute of Education in London, I learn that they explained that even before the 18th century, farm land had been enclosed in about two-fifths of all the villages in England, and that after 1760, "the richer farmers and gentlemen in thousands of villages petitioned Parliament, and forced the poorer people to have the land enclosed. The rule was that if the people who owned four-fifths of the land wanted it divided and enclosed, they could get what they wanted, no matter what other people said."[3] The text went on to explain why so many small farmers and cottagers were ruined. The author's account was a skilful retelling for the child reader, of the version of the history of enclosure from *The Village Labourer* by J.L. and Barbara Hammond, first published in 1911. When I was a secondary school pupil in the late 1930s, the book used was G.W. Southgate's *Textbook of Modern English History* which explained that in rural England, "Consolidation and enclosure were absolutely necessary. It does not follow that the reform was carried out in the best possible way."[5]

After the second world war, the Hammond book was re-issued as two cheap paperbacks, and I read it for the first time, overwhelmed by the mountain of local detail that they had assembled. The authors were then still living and had contributed a preface to that 1948 reprint. Firstly it drew attention to the criticism of their book when it first appeared, as here it had been argued

> "in the first place that the picture given of the enclo-sures was unjust, because the writers deliberately excluded the importance of enclosure in increasing the food supplies of the nation, and, in the second, that the hardships of the poor had been exagger-ated, and that, though the system of enclosure lent itself to abuses, there was no evidence that wrong was done in the case of enclosures."[6]

They responded with two observations. The first was that, if agriculture had suddenly become so astonishingly productive, shouldn't its labourers have had some bene-fit? "The greater the stress laid upon the progress of agri-culture, the greater appear the perversity and injustice of the arrangement of a society under which the labourer was impoverished." Their second objection was equally apposite. It had been contended that their account of the hardships of the poor had been exaggerated, and they claimed that, on the contrary, their book had described the way that, not only the best qualified observers at the time, like Arthur Young and William Cobbett, but also even "the Committees that examined the methods of enclosure remarked on the absence of any provision for the special protection of the poor." Talking of the absence of recorded opposition to enclosures, they stressed that "The only consents of which Committees took account were those of persons with rights of property: the great mass of cottagers did not fall into this category. They would therefore never come into the pages of the Commons' *Journals.*"[7]

141

My own mentor, George Southgate, made a similar point:

> "In every manor in which the old system survived there was a considerable stretch of open pasture, or common, on which the peasants were entitled by custom to graze their cattle and sheep, and a few acres of woodland on which fuel could be obtained and timber cut. Though the country folk could show no legal right to these privileges they had existed from time immemorial, and nobody thought of challenging them..."[8]

He went on to explain that "the peasant who received a plot of a few acres found himself worse off than he was before" not only because he had no longer any place to graze his plough-oxen, his pigs or his poultry, but because he had no capital to meet the cost of enclosing his patch with a hedge or fence. "In his bewilderment he was ready to accept the first reasonable offer that was made for his small property. Offers were not lacking."[9]

A long series of scholars have, since then, examined the effect of the enclosures, correcting or refining each others' conclusions, and coping with subtleties beyond the scope of schoolbooks. One of them, Professor Gordon Mingay, observed in the 1970s that "the 'Hammond version' of the parliamentary enclosure movement of eighteenth-century England is still extensively taught in the schoolrooms of this country after more than sixty years."[10] But later historians, including Mingay, had contradicted the Hammond version, using words of the kind that Keith Snell gathered from the writings of Gordon Mingay himself, describing it as 'mistaken', 'exaggerated', 'overdrawn', 'unrealistic', 'unhistorical', 'partial and tendentious', 'seriously astray', 'biased' and 'illiberal'.[11] They took the view that the changes resulting from enclosure were historically inevitable in order to produce the new urban working class through migration, as well as to make possible an increase in the productivity of agriculture, which had been hampered not only by the archaic system of the common fields, but also by the cotters' and squatters' colonisation of the 'wastes' where, as Griffiths Cunningham put it, "vast stretches of the English countryside were 'no-man's-land' in the real sense of the word,"[12] provided a livelihood for an almost hidden population of otherwise landless peasants.

Professors Mingay and Chambers argued that the changes in agriculture resulting from enclosure after 1750 were a desirable revolution in which British agriculture fed 6.5 million more people by 1850, thus avoiding the 'Malthusian check' by which the growth of population outstripped increases in food production. But a later series of scholars have provided locally detailed evidence that reinforces the 'Hammond version' One of them, the same Dr Snell, argues that the most recent reappraisal of open-field agriculture has established that "the open fields were far more open to innovative and flexible agriculture than was once supposed", and that "the account of them as seriously backward and by nature inhibitive of new techniques is most certainly incorrect."[14]

The Hammonds had claimed that enclosure was fatal to three classes of rural dwellers; the small farmer, the cottager, and the squatter. But of course the three had differing interests, although they were at one in finding it difficult or impossible to meet their allocated share of the costs of an enclosure award and the cost of fencing. Not all villagers were able to establish a claim to land or to common rights in the unenclosed village, and of course squatters were the most vulnerable of the villagers. Discussing "The Disappearance of the Cottager and the Squatter from the English Countryside", J.V. Beckett observes that

"Squatters were not necessarily unwelcome when there was plenty of common land. At Myddle, in Shropshire, 236½ acres of common were still available in 1813, and with such plentiful grazing there seem never to have been any restrictions. But circumstances could change. Friction occurred when too many people (some of them genuine squatters attracted by the availability of unstinted commons) wanted to run too many animals on the common. The solution adopted was usually stinting; in other

Cottage at the end of Myddlewood, Shropshire, which W.G. Hoskins found "had become a distinctive squatters' colony by the end of the 17th century." Built by John Hughes, it was originally "only one bay in length and open to the rafters. Another bay was added (to left of picture), *then a brick chimney was inserted and upper chambers installed." Hoskins found that the cottage belonged to another labouring family, the Hammers, for most of the 17th century. "Ellis Hammer had arrived in the parish in 1581 when he built a one-bay cottage nearby. Such meagre accommodation was, however, better than that of his neighbour, Thomas Chidlow, a labourer who lived in 'a poore pitifull hut, built up to an old oake'."*
(PHOTO: LEICESTER UNIVERSITY PRESS).

words restrictions were introduced on the number of animals (and what type) any individual might run on the commons. This was what happened at Willingham in Cambridgeshire. As a result of the growth of the village by the 1650s the villagers were frequently to be found arguing over the unequal use of the commons. Four non-resident gentlemen were invited to arbitrate in the disputes by producing an agreeable stint..."[15]

The Hammonds themselves had noted how in Enclosure awards the treatment of encroachments seems to have varied very greatly:

"and there was no settled rule. Squatters of less than twenty years' standing seldom received any consideration beyond the privilege of buying their encroachment. Squatters of more than twenty or forty years' standing, as the case might be, were often allowed to keep their encroachments, and in some cases were treated like cottagers, with a claim to an allotment. But, of course, like the cottagers, they lost their common rights."[16]

Gordon Mingay found that all those labourers who could produce a sound claim to their land or common rights were compensated by the enclosure commissioners, "though whether the compensation was adequate is another matter", but he added that

"there were many whose access to the common arose from occupation of an ancient cottage or tenement, not from ownership, and it was the owner, not the tenant who was entitled to receive the compensation decided by the commissioners. And there was a further group of cottagers and squatters whose use of the common was on a purely customary basis: in some instance they had merely assumed a right and in others they had been permitted to use the common as a concession by those who held the established rights."[17]

He found that, if enquiry among the oldest inhabitants showed that a claimant had used the common without hindrance "for twenty or sometimes forty years, or for 'time out of mind', then the claim would be accepted." And he added that "certainly the commissioners disallowed many customary claims because they were challenged by other villagers and on examination were found to fail the test applied."[18]

The most recent, and splendidly detailed study of the rights and the economy of commoners, cotters and squatters alike, is Professor Jeanette Neeson's account of the co-operative regulation of common fields and pastures, and the harvests taken from uncultivated common waste, *Commoners*. She provides in rich detail, evidence of the ways in which common rights could double a family income, describing how

"Living off the produce of commons encouraged frugality, economy, thrift. Productive commons had always been the insurance, the reserves, the hidden wealth of commoners — they were the oldest part of an ancient economy. They gave commoners the fuel, food and materials that kept them out of the market for labour and out of the market for consumption too. And the more productive the common, the more independent the commoners,

"The habit of living off commons made the habit of regular employment less necessary. For commoners it was customary to make a living first out of the materials on hand; after all, the commons came first, wage labour was a relatively recent arrival. This is not to deny the existence of wage labour; earning wages was necessary, but until they became the lion's share of income they were supplementary, not central to a commoning economy."[20]

There were also, of course, landless commoners, who owned or rented no land and whose cottages "did not entitle them to compensation for loss of common right". Professor Neeson notes that "In some parishes immigrants and squatters were also landless commoners."[21] Other historians would see the difference between cottagers and squatters as simply a matter of length of residence. Hence the careful regard, noted in the researches of Dr Moir quoted in Chapter 8, given by cottagers to their bequests as legitimising evidence. One historian, J.V. Beckett, asked the key question: How many squatters were there? But he was obliged to answer that "Even those who have studied the subject in detail have found quantification almost impossible"[22] He, like me, is obliged to gather up anecdotal evidence from a series of local accounts, starting by observing that

"Squatters are rather more difficult to identify because of the way in which they arrived in a community. Wherever land was only semi-cleared the spacious commons and wastes attracted landless migrants. If commons were unstinted anyone could set up a cottage and enjoy the benefits. Individuals could erect a home of some sort on the edges of heaths and commons; indeed, it was widely believed that a cottage erected on the waste overnight entitled its builder to undisputed possession..."[23]

Looking for some quantification, Professor Beckett adds that,

"Writing of sixteenth-century Shropshire David Hey could be no more precise than to discuss 'large numbers of squatters who began to erect cottages on the edges of the commons and unproductive land.' Slightly firmer evidence comes from the Derbyshire Peak where opportunities in lead mining encouraged squatting. There were thirty squatters at

147

Wirksworth in 1649, and ten or more in a number of other parishes during the 1650s. In the West Midlands ninety-nine cottages had encroached on the wastes at West Bromwich by 1793, and from Walsall and Bloxwith it was reported in 1763 that forty-two acres had been taken in by 211 separate encroachments."[24]

The same kind of local testimony was cited by Dennis Mills, describing how "in some areas squatting went well beyond the surreptitious cottage or two. The rapid rise of population in the parishes of Windsor Forest (1676 — estimated 4,715; 1801 — 13,065) was attributed very considerably to unlicensed cottages. Similarly Enfield Chase gained about a hundred squatter houses in the period 1670-1700, where there was said to be an abundance of loose, idle and disorderly persons. Squatting was also said to be extensive in east Suffolk."[25] Mills goes on to summarise the study of the Weald of Sussex by Peter Brandon, describing how

"Hundreds of smallholdings and cottages are reported to have been scattered indiscriminately across Wealden wastes such as the Heathfield-Burwash-Battle and Ashdown Forest areas. The permission of manorial lords was sometimes given, but more often one reads of attempts to get rid of squatters' cottages or to curtail their numbers..."[26]

The attempt to answer the question 'How many squatters were there?' is made virtually impossible, not only by the geographical distribution of squatter dwellings, but by the continuous process of legitimisation over time. Just as it was a routine procedure for a manor court to impose a fine which then became a rent, and was usually levied at the level which it was assumed that the squatter could pay, so there have for centuries been rules of thumb for the length of unchallenged occupation of a site that established 'squatter's rights' — a term not recognised by the law which was sometimes 40 years, but more usually 20, and more recently, twelve. Squatter cottages were cold, leaky and damp, as could be predicted about the homes improvised by the poor, but the terrible truth about the history of rural life is that the legitimately provided homes of farm workers, whether 'tied' cottages provided by employers, or rented cottages in the village, were no better. An endless series of reports on the living conditions of the rural poor provided testimony of the unwillingness of the landowning minority of the rural population to improve the living conditions of the landless majority.[27]

As the 19th century moved on, the process of enclosure became rarer, when the costs for landlords began to outweigh the benefits. A long period of depression was followed by the prosperity of "high farming" as machinery began to displace labour, but then by the agricultural depression that lasted, with a few upturns like 1916-19, from 1875 until the second world war. As cheap wheat and frozen or tinned meat were imported from all over the globe, there was a vast exodus of the rural poor, to the cities and to the then British dominions, colonies and protectorates.

The experience of the 19th century poor in the Scottish Highlands and Islands, was characterised by experiences worse than those inflicted by the most ruthless of English landlords. In the parishes studied by James Hunter in his study of *The Making of the Crofting Community*, about a quarter of all resident families were landless and were subsumed under the generic title of 'cottars and squatters.' (It is not strictly true but we can assume that the word 'cottar' is Scottish and the word 'cotter' English). James Hunter explains that:

"The former, in technical terms, were the inhabitants of dwellings built on holdings whose officially recognised occupants were usually close relatives of the cottars concerned while the latter usually lived in houses built on the edge of a township's common grazings. Cottars generally cultivated a part of the croft on which they resided and occasionally paid a share of the rent. Squatters, however, paid no rent, despite the fact that they had frequently brought a part of common pasture into cultivation. Because their position was utterly insecure and their very existence a violation of estate regulations, precise numbers of cottars and squatters are difficult to determine. Equally hard to determine is the point at which the lowliest crofters became cottars — a fact which led the Napier Commissioners to observe, correctly, that the distinction between the two groups was 'more easily felt than delineated'."[28]

In Scotland, the land-owning classes adapted ruthless measures against rural over-population, because in their view, the poor "bred like rabbits". Their own lifestyle and the ways in which they sought to profit from the sporting potential of their vast holdings, needed a dependent, servant class, but not whole colonies of waged employees.

But in England, by the end of the nineteenth century, the land-owning classes had become worried by the spectre of rural depopulation. Their worries (the subject of endless humour in journals like *Punch*, became known as "the servant problem", and a dozen studies were undertaken into the possibility of the repopulation of rural England and Wales.[29] The poor were unaffected by this, and encouraged their children to leave the village. They were bound, not merely for British towns and cities, but for Canada, South Africa, Australia or New Zealand — any of the territories seized by British imperialism, where their chance of a better life was far greater than in the villages of their birth. There everything belonged to someone else, and no amount of ingenuity or hard work would improve the condition of the families known to their betters as 'village people.'

In the journal *The Nineteenth Century*, the anarchist propagandist Peter Kropotkin was providing in the last years of that century, his account of leaving London with a knapsack on his back and tramping through the empty landscape. He started in Surrey and ended in South Devon where he reported that

> "field after field is covered with nothing but grass, three inches high, and thistles in profusion. Twenty, thirty such fields can be seen at one glance from the top of every hill; and thousands of acres are in that state, notwithstanding that the grandfathers of the present generation have devoted a formidable amount of labour to the clearing of that land. In every direction I see abandoned cottages and orchards going to ruin. A whole population has disappeared... And this takes place in a part of the country endowed with a more fertile soil and possessed of a climate which is certainly more congenial than the climate of Jersey in spring and early summer — a land upon which even the poorest cottagers occasionally raised potatoes as early as the first half of May. But how can land be cultivated when there is nobody to cultivate it?"[30]

Precisely a century after this account was written, the fields were empty again. Fifty years of subsidies had made the owners of arable land millionaires through mechanised cultivation, and with a crisis of over-production the European Community was rewarding them for growing no crops on part of their land. In 1995, a total of 544,900 hectares, 5.9 per cent of the entire farmed area of England was set aside in this way.[31]

However, opportunities for the homeless poor were fewer than ever in history.

References

1. Tom Williamson and Liz Bellamy *Property and Landscape: a social history of land ownership and the English country-side*, London: George Philip 1987 p.102.
2. Herbert Read: "The Open Fields System" *Spain and the World* Supplement December 1938 discussing C.S. and C.S. Orwin *The Open Fields*, Oxford: Clarendon Press 1938. Review reprinted in David Goodway (ed) Herbert Read *A One-Man Manifesto*, London: Freedom Press 1994, pp. 40-43.
3. E.H. Spalding *Piers Plowman Histories Junior Book V*, London: George Philip 1929, p.192.
4. J.L. and Barbara Hammond *The Village Labourer 1760-1832*, London: Longmans 1911.
5. George W. Southgate *A Text Book of Modern English History Section III*, London: J.M. Dent 1930, p.4.
6. J.L. and Barbara Hammond "Preface to the Guild Edition" of *The Village Labourer*, London: Guild Books 1948 p.6.
7. *ibid* p.7.
8. G.W. Southgate *op cit* p.2.
9. *ibid* p.5.
10. Gordon Mingay "General Introduction" to 1978 edition of J.L. and B. Hammond: *The Village Labourer,* London: Longmans 1978 p.viii.
11. K.D.M. Snell *Annals of the Labouring Poor: Social Change and Agrarian England 1660-1900*, Cambridge University Press 1985 p.141.
12. Griffiths Cunningham "Early Allotment Garden History" Unpublished paper 1986.
13. J.D. Chambers and G.E. Mingay *The Agricultural Revolution, 1750-1880,* London: B.T. Batsford 1966.
14. K.D.M. Snell op cit pp. 104-5
15. J.V. Beckett "The Disappearance of the Cottager and the Squatter from the English Countryside: The Hammonds Revisited" in B.A. Holderness and Michael Turner (eds) *Land, Labour and Agriculture, 1700-1920: Essays for Gordon Mingay*, London: The Hambledon Press 1991, p.55.
16. J.L. and Barbara Hammond *op cit* 1948 edition Vol 1 pp. 98-99.
17. Gordon Mingay "General Introduction" *op cit* p.xx.
18. *ibid.*
19. J.M. Neeson *Commoners: common right, enclosure and social change in England, 1700-1820*, Cambridge University Press 1993.
20. *ibid* p.177.

152

21. *ibid* p.64.
22. J.V. Beckett *op cit* p.54.
23. *ibid* citing Joan Thirsk (ed) *The Agrarian History of England and Wales, Vol 4, 1500-1640*, Cambridge University Press 1967, p.445.
24. *ibid* citing D.G. Hey *An English Rural Community: Myddle under the Tudors and Stuarts*, Leicester University Press 1974, p.10, and Joan Thirsk (ed) *The Agrarian History of England and Wales, Vol 5, 1, 1640-1750* Cambridge University Press 1984, pp. 135, 145.
25. Dennis R. Mills *Lord and Peasant in Nineteenth Century Britain*, London: Croom Helm 1900, p.102.
26. *ibid* pp. 102-3, citing Peter Brandon *The Sussex Landscape*, London: Hodder and Stoughton 1974, pp. 194-8.
27. See for example John Burnett *A Social History of Housing 1815-1970*, London: Allen Lane 1978, Enid Gauldie *Cruel Habitations*, London: Allen & Unwin 1974.
28. James Hunter *The Making of the Crofting Community*, Edinburgh: John Donald 1976, new edition 2000, p.179.
29. The novelist and landowner H. Rider Haggard was commissioned by the government to write *The Poor and the Land*, London: Longmans, Green 1905, and in the previous decade William Booth of the Salvation Army had written *In Darkest England, and the Way Out*, (1890), the socialist Robert Blatchford had written *Merrie England*, (1893) which sold a million copies by the end of the century.
30. Peter Kropotkin *Fields, Factories and Workshops* (1899) New edition, ed. Colin Ward, London: Allen & Unwin 1974, Freedom Press reprint 1985 p.54.
31. Peter Hall and Colin Ward *Sociable Cities: the legacy of Ebenezer Howard*, Chichester: John Wiley & Sons 1990 p.107.

Chapter 13
Plotters and squatters
of the 20th century

"A combination of cheap land and transport, prefab-
ricated materials, and the owner's labour and skills
had given back to the ordinary people of the land, the
opportunity denied to them for over two hundred
years, an opportunity which, at the time, was still
available to almost half of the world's non-industri-
alised population: the freedom for a man to build his
own house. It was a freedom that was to be very
short-lived,"

Anthony King: *The Bungalow: A Global History*[1]

All through the first half of the 20th century, British agriculture was sunk in a depression that lasted until the
introduction of government support with guaranteed
prices in 1939 (with a brief respite from 1916 until the end
of the first world war because of the loss of shipping
importing food). Rural land-owning had become, in the
eyes of the land-owners, a liability rather than an asset.
The exceptions were, of course, the really big aristocratic
families with vast holdings of urban land, mineral rights,
or with lucrative marriages to the daughters of industrial
millionaires.

Land which had been the subject of bitterly-contested
enclosure battles, dispossessing cottagers, commoners and
small farmers a century earlier, was sold to whoever made
an offer in the 1920s. As Howard Newby explained,

"In four years between 1918 and 1922 England, in
the words of a famous *Times* leader of the day,
'changed hands'. One quarter of the area of England
was bought and sold in this hectic period of transac-

tion, a disposal of land which was unprecedented since the dissolution of the monasteries in the six-teenth century,"[2]

The word 'plotlands' was later devised by planners and conservation bodies to describe those areas of former farmland where, as one bankruptcy followed another, and as the willingness of migrating Scottish and Welsh farmers who were seeking a place to make good slowly evaporated, estate agents and speculators had devised other markets. They sought to sell fields in small plots where city-dwellers could, for a trivial sum, buy the site for their week-end or retirement home, chicken farm, chalet or holiday shanty. Sites were advertised in pubs and local papers and on the backs of tram tickets issued by the London County Council.

By 1939 this plotland landscape was to be found in pockets across the North Downs, across the Hampshire plain, and along the Thames Valley at sites like Penton Hook, Marlow Bottom and Purley Park. It was interspersed among the established holiday resorts of East and West Sussex at places like Shoreham Beach, Pett Level, Dungeness and Camber Sands, and, famously, at Peacehaven. It crept up the East Coast, from Sheppey in Kent to Lincolnshire, by way of Canvey Island and Jaywick Sands, and it clustered inland all across south Essex. There is an invisible geological line, running across the county of Essex, dividing the clay that farmers used to call two-horse land, from the thicker kind they knew as three-horse land which went out of use earlier.

When Dennis Hardy and I gathered together the story of the plotlands of South-East England in our book *Arcadia for All*[3] we were conscious that we had been just in time to question the survivors from the first generation of these new country dwellers. Sometimes our conversations revealed that they themselves were only one generation removed from rural life. Their own parents had left the village for the East End of London in the agricultural depression of the late 19th century, and they had used a free rail trip from Fenchurch Street station to South Essex, to pay £5 at an open-air auction for a plot on which to erect, first of all, a second-hand army tent. Often only a pound was paid as a deposit on the title deeds, the rest to be paid in monthly installments. We had confined ourselves to the south-east of England and the London hinterland, but the plotland phenomenon was not confined to the south-east. Every industrial conurbation in Britain once had these escape routes to the country, river or sea. For the West Midlands there was the Severn Valley or North Wales, for Liverpool and Manchester, places in the Wirral, for Glasgow, the Ayrshire coast and even the banks of Loch Lomond, for the West Riding towns and cities, the Yorkshire coast and the Humber estuary, and for those of Tyneside and Teesside, the coasts of Northumberland and Durham.

It is as though a proportion of the population felt obliged to follow some ancient human habit in seeking out some place, however hard to find, where people could build for themselves. There are parallels of course with the 'chalet gardens' — the combination of allotment gardens and holiday cottages which are part of the culture of urban life in the Netherlands and the Scandinavian countries. When David Crouch and I were writing the history of the culture of the allotment, we found disbelief in other countries that spending the week-end on the allotment was a notion regarded with horror by British local authorities and completely outlawed.[4] But the most suggestive comparison is with urban life in the former Soviet empire countries like Poland, Hungary, Czechoslovakia or Bulgaria, where the residents of city blocks of flats exercise endless ingenuity in finding a patch of land out of town which evolves from an allotment garden into a second home, or *dacha*, and ultimately to the place perceived as the family base, to which the week-day city flat is secondary.[5]

In Britain, the spread of plots and settlements across derelict farmland aroused horror among right-thinking and privileged people. They were seen as a blot on the landscape and a sanitary menace (since they failed to comply with the building by-laws), and their existence was a major factor in winning support for the comprehensive system of development control that has existed in Britain since the post-war Town and Country Planning Act. Plotland development was outlawed, and some planning authorities sought to eliminate them. On most sites they evolved through the usual processes of improvement over time into ordinary suburban housing, hidden in woodland. As everything is eventually sanctified as history, several plotland sites have been designated as Conservation Areas, and one of them, at Basildon in Essex, has a Plotland Museum.[6]

The plotland settlers were quite often described as squatters, with the word being used as a term of abuse. It was, in fact, inaccurate since most had paid for their sites at what was the highest price that the sellers could obtain. But when, in south Essex, a plot was bought for a one pound deposit and four further monthly installments, the seller lacked the clerical staff to chase the missing pound, so title to the site might be dubious, but was eventually validated by time and undisputed possession. The developer of Peacehaven on the South Coast, Charles Neville, staged a competition in which thousands of entrants were told that they had won a free plot, but were asked to pay three guineas for legal fees for the transfer of the land. "Sceptics were quick to point out that at a purchase cost of £15 per acre and with a 'conveyancing charge' equivalent to more than £47 per acre, even allowing for minimal expenses, Neville stood to gain a profit in the region of £30 for every acre."[7] The case ended in court and the judge concluded that the plots were absolutely worthless and that the scheme was no more than a clever fraud. When I discussed the developer's reputation in 1980 with Mrs Sayers, a Peacehaven resident for sixty years, she responded with the observation that she and her husband had found opportunities in settling there, which were denied them everywhere else.[8]

At the end of the second world war the concept of squatting was given a new emphasis. No new houses had been built in Britain for six years, while there was a vast number of new families, and the age at which young people found partners had lowered significantly. Demobilised members of the armed forces were desperate to get away from overcrowded parental households. In May 1946 large numbers of families began to occupy empty military camps. Aneurin Bevan, the Minister of Health (then the department of government responsible for housing) sought to turn public feeling against the camp squatters by suggesting that they were "Jumping their places in the housing queue", although in fact they were jumping out of the queues by moving into buildings which would not otherwise have been used for housing purposes. In September, Aneurin Bevan, back from his holiday in Switzerland, instructed local authorities to cut off gas and electricity supplies to property occupied by squatters, but in October the government announced that 1,038 camps in England and Wales had been occupied by 39,535 people, and began to urge local authorities to install families in military camps.[9] By this time local councils were already directing homeless families to occupy huts in camps where the unofficial settlers were already organising communal cooking and nursery facilities and forming a rota to stoke the boilers left behind by the armed forces. Early in 1947 a newspaper correspondent provided a very revealing report from a Lancashire camp:

"There are two camps within the camp — the official squatters (that is, people who have been placed in the huts after the first invasion) and the unofficial squatters (the veterans who have been allowed to remain on sufferance). Both pay the same rent of 10 shillings a week — but there the similarity ends. Although one would have imagined that the acceptance of rent from both should accord them identical privileges, in fact it does not. Workmen have put up partitions in the huts of the official squatters and have put in sinks and numerous other conveniences. These are the sheep; the goats have perforce to fend for themselves.

"An interesting commentary on the situation was made by one of the young welfare officers attached to the housing department. On her visit of inspection she found that the goats had set to work with a will, improvising partitions, running up curtains, distempering, painting and using initiative. The official squatters on the other hand, sat about glumly without lifting a hand to help themselves and bemoaning their fate, even though they might have been removed from the most appalling slum property. Until the overworked corporation workmen got around to them they would not attempt to improve affairs themselves."[10]

Meanwhile, as the camps began to fill, squatters turned to other empty buildings: hotels, shops, mansions, disused schools, race tracks and a stadium were among the places occupied. The most spectacular phase of the 1946 campaign of urban squatting was the occupation of a series of hotels and luxury flats which had been requisitioned for wartime use and were now empty. Police attitudes to the squatters varied from day to day from sympathy to threats, according to their instructions from the Home Office. Described in the press as a Communist stunt, the wave of squatting ended with a 'general evacuation' by the London squatters when a High Court injunction against them was granted.

Local authorities found accommodation of one kind or another for the urban squatters, while the camp settlers had settled down until they could find something better. Urban squatting continued quietly, especially as local councils acquired vast tracts of urban housing and left it empty for eventual comprehensive redevelopment. It re-emerged as a public issue in 1968 thanks to two activists,

Ron Bailey and Jim Radford, who had been busy agitating against the failure of local authorities to comply with their statutory duty to the homeless, trying after long and bitter campaigns to draw public attention to conditions in hostels for homeless families. By this time, as Bailey put it, "a squatting campaign was clearly on the cards; it only needed a spark to set it off."[11] They installed homeless families in unoccupied houses which had been publicly acquired and earmarked for demolition years later for eventual road improvements, car parking or municipal offices.

Local authorities responded violently, using so-called 'bailiffs' to intimidate squatting families and using their own employees to wreck the interiors of empty houses to keep the squatters out. Widely reported in the press and on television, these activities brought public sympathy for the squatters. Several London boroughs entered into legal agreements for accepting squatters as tenants, with the result as Bailey later put it that "tens of thousands of homes that would otherwise have stayed empty have been brought back into use and hundreds of thousands of homeless people given new hope and dignity."[12]

Municipal politicians have come to agreements with squatters (and this is perhaps more evident in other European cities like Amsterdam and Copenhagen), but central government politicians of both major parties in Britain have been unremittingly hostile. Once they discovered that squatting was seen as a civil, rather than a criminal offence, and was governed by legislation dating back to the year 1381, they set about changing the situation. The Law Commission responded in 1974 with a document on Criminal Law Offences of Entering and Remaining on Property, which was incorporated into legislation by the Criminal Law Act of 1977. This failed to deter the country's 50,000 or so squatters, and in practice, so did its successor, the Criminal Justice Act of 1994.

In preparation for this Act, the Home Office issued a Consultation Paper in which it stated that it "does not accept the claim that squatting results from social deprivation. Squatters are generally there by their own choice, moved by no more than self-gratification or an unreadiness to respect other people's rights." (Para 62). It also observed that cases of squatting "involving young children were negligible." (Para 9).[13] But in the year when the Act became law, Ron Bailey used the latest available survey figures to show that the facts were different. He found that,

"About one third of squatting households contain children and this has been the case for over five years. Under Section 58 of the Housing Act of 1985 all such families are statutorily homeless and so entitled to be accommodated by local authorities. The fact they they are squatting actually saves ratepayers vast amounts of money. Many other squatters need psychiatric help, since 1990 more than 28,000 hospital beds have been lost and only 5,000 residential places provided. Thus, many ill people have drifted into sleeping rough and squatting. In addition, currently 2,000 squatters are women escaping violent partners. Even more squatters are homeless single people for whom there is no statutory provision at all and for whom council waiting lists are meaningless. About one in twenty squatters (2,500 people) are ex-owner occupiers, evicted as they were unable to meet mortgage repayments. In conclusion, therefore, all the available evidence shows that squatters are homeless people in desperate housing need, often with other social problems such as mental illness or the need to escape violence and harassment. These are the people that the government is attempting to make into criminals."[14]

In shifting the act of squatting from the category of a civil offence to that of a criminal action, successive Home

Secretaries of both major parties reflected the fears of readers of the popular press that they might return from holidays and find strangers sleeping in their beds. The reality is different. The overwhelming majority of squatted buildings had been empty for years and had been the subject of a compulsory purchase order from a department of central or local government for a vast project: new roads, housing or hospital-building, which, through a change of policy failed to happen. People like Ron Bailey persuaded some local authorities to make these houses available for 'short-life housing co-ops' and some of those co-ops have had a very long life.

Other such houses have been in the unchallenged occupation of squatters for so long that they have chosen to secure their future by claiming what is still known as 'squatter's rights'. As the law stands, under the provisions of the Limitation Act of 1980, a squatter can gain title to land or premises through 'adverse possession' if he has been in unchallenged possession for 12 years. A great deal of publicity has been given to a handful of cases in south London where squatters have succeeded in gaining title in this way.[15]

Not far away was Tenants' Corner, an old shop acquired for a redevelopment that never happened and which lay empty until it was occupied as a meeting place for tenant groups when the Thatcher government began compelling local authorities to dispose of public housing. It had an important role in the campaign for tenant co-operatives. As I knew that they had been the occupiers for longer than the statutory period, I asked the people running Tenants' Corner whether they intended to claim possession. "Of course not," was their reply. "Why should we join the queue to make a private profit from public assets?"

The instances of claims for 'adverse possession' that actually reach the courts tend to arise when one land occupier seeks payment from another for the right of access across a particular piece of forgotten land. In 1994 a Suffolk businessman published a book called *How to*

Claim Land and Houses in the UK, remarking that "It sounds unbelievable, but there are millions of pounds waiting to be made."[16]

The last decade of the 20th century witnessed two interesting examples of creative squatting. The first was Exodus in Bedfordshire. This grew out of the 'rave' culture of instant large-scale overnight music festivals.

> "On 4 January 1993, Exodus supported fourteen homeless people who had squatted a long-empty property in Luton, the Oakmore Hotel. Money from bucket collections at the parties helped renovate the derelict property... On 15 January police raided and severely damaged the Oakmore Hotel... Six weeks after the initial police raid, the Oakmore was evicted during a snow storm. The occupants were given half an hour to leave. St Margaret's Hospice, a derelict old people's home, was immediately occupied. Exodus were eventually granted a lease, and renamed the property HAZ Manor, Housing Action Zone Manor. People pay their rent/housing benefit into a communal pot, which is used to renovate the building. Decisions are reached by consensus rather than majority rule at collective meetings. Space has been created for some forty people to live there now, with their own rooms and a communal kitchen and living areas. Workshops are being built, crafts learned. It's a big miracle, a beacon of Do-it-Ourselves help."[17]

Tim Malyon, who watched and enthused over this "history of reclaiming territory for the dispossessed", went on to describe the next step in the evolution of Exodus. One of the party venues for rave parties initiated by Exodus was Longmeadow Farm. In the days of continuous compulsory purchase by the Department of Transport for new roads (in this case the widening of the M1) the farm had been acquired and then left to rot. Exodus, Tim Malyon explains, squatted the farm and was eventually offered a lease by the DOT. As at HAZ Manor, the buildings and a house and bungalow were renovated, with a busy use of wood recycled from donated pallets, and a herd of animals was acquired.[18] Before the end of the century there were new efforts by government departments to evict Exodus.[18]

The second of these end of century campaigns was the attempt to put the issue of the right of access to land back on the popular agenda in Britain with a network of propagandist groups called *The Land is Ours*.[19] Its first manifestation was the invasion of a site near St George's Hill in Surrey, where Winstanley's Diggers had squatted in 1949, and this was followed in May 1996 by the occupation of a long-empty site on the banks of the Thames at Wandsworth in London. This derelict industrial land was of thirteen acres (5.2 hectares), and the local planning authority had rejected one superstore proposal after another, on the grounds that they contributed nothing to the locality. The campaigners submitted a planning application pressing the claims for a new urban village of do-it-yourself homes and gardens. Five hundred activists settled on the site in May 1996 in a glare of publicity and began to put up shacks and shanties, tents and yurts. They cleared rubbish and planted gardens. It fell to me on the third day of the occupation to be the invited speaker describing the hidden history of squatter housing, talking in a building that had not existed a day before.

One of the people supporting me there was the late Eric Mattocks, a founder and treasurer of the Advisory Service for Squatters, bringing with him, straight from the press, the tenth edition of the *Squatters Handbook*.[20] It was he who had negotiated with the Greater London Council, the amnesty of 1978, in which about 12,000 squatters in council-owned property, were given authorised tenancies, and he sought to stress that squatting was not merely a demonstration, it was an initiator of social change. The owners of the site, Guinness, held back for five and a half months, and at dawn on 15 October 1996, employed bailiffs supported by nearly 250 policemen in riot gear to drive out the squatters. The occupation of the site, known as Gargoyle Wharf, had served to re-awaken interest in Britain in the issue of urban land and its uses.

References

1. Anthony King *The Bungalow: a global history*, London: Routledge & Kegan Paul 1984.
2. Howard Newby *Green and Pleasant Land?* London: Hutchinson 1979.
3. Dennis Hardy and Colin Ward *Arcadia for All: the legacy of a makeshift landscape*, London: Mansell 1984.
4. David Crouch and Colin Ward *The Allotment: its landscape and culture*, London: Faber & Faber 1988 p.142.
5. *ibid* p.150.
6. Hardy and Ward *op cit.* pp. 209-210.
7. *ibid* pp. 74 75.
8. *ibid* pp. 90-91.
9. Colin Ward "Direct Action for houses: the story of the squatters" *Anarchy* Vol 3 No 1, January 1963, pp. 9-15.
10. "How Are They Now?" *News Chronicle* 14 January 1947.
11. Ron Bailey *The Squatters*, Harmondsworth: Penguin Books 1973.
12. Ron Bailey *Homelessness: what can be done*, Oxford: Jon Carpenter 1994, p.iii.
13. Home Office *Consultation Paper on Squatting*, London: Home Office 1993.
14. Ron Bailey *Homelessness op cit* p.94.
15. "Squatter made legal owner of £200,000 council house" *Daily Telegraph* 21 July 1999.
16. "Laying claim to houses and land no one owns" *East Anglian Daily Times* 11 July 1994.
17. Tim Malyon "Tossed in the fire and they never got burned: the Exodus Collective" in George McKay *DIY Culture: party & protest in nineties Britain*, London: Verso 1998 pp. 187-207.
18. *ibid* p.204
19. *The Land is Ours*, 16b Cherwell Street, Oxford OX4 1BG.
20. *Squatters Handbook*, Tenth Edition London: Advisory Service for Squatters, 2 St Paul's Road, London N1, May 1996.

Chapter 14
The land is whose?

"Hardly noticed at first, 'Property is Theft' was to become one of the great phrases of the nineteenth century, bandied about between anarchists and conservatives, borrowed by socialists and communists, and suspended like a sensational placard above the popular image of its author. Ironically enough, Proudhon did not even mean literally what he said. His boldness of expression was intended for emphasis... He was denouncing the property of the man who uses it to exploit the labour of others without any effort on his own part, the property that is distinguished by interest, usury and rent, by the impositions of the non-producer upon the producer. Towards property regarded as 'possession', the right of a man to control his dwelling and the land and tools he needed to work and live, Proudhon had no hostility; he regarded it as a necessary keystone of liberty, and his main criticism of the Communists was that they wished to destroy it."

George Woodcock *Pierre-Joseph Proudhon: A Biography*[1]

In September 1969 we all cheered when Proudhon's phrase *Property is Theft* was placarded in letters three feet high on the walls of 144 Piccadilly in London, a former royal residence. The squatters were evicted and the slogan removed. And as the Crown and the royal family owns more of Britain than anyone else, Proudhon's slogan had an unqualified and unequivocal appropriateness, obvious to all.

But of course, there has always been a distinction between squatting as a political demonstration, from that

167

of Winstanley and the Diggers at St George's Hill in Surrey in 1649 to that of *The Land is Ours* at Wandsworth in 1996, and squatting as a personal solution to a housing problem. In the first instance the intention is, for propagandist purposes, to be noticed. In the second, the hope is to be inconspicuous and to blend into the landscape. Given the public perception of the squatters' movement, it has always been a paradox that, just as the Herefordshire village squatters yearned to establish their children's rights in their wills, so the typical modern squatter actually hopes for the security of a rent book.

Theoretical revolutionaries may be disappointed by the gulf between rhetoric and daily life because of a curious inability to distinguish between the property of the landlord and that of the peasant. "No man," urged Winstanley, "shall have any more land than he can labour himself, or have others to labour with him in love, working together and eating bread together,"[2] and this is precisely the difference between the appropriation of land by squatters and that by enclosers.

Many cultures share the tradition that the land was once the common property of the people. "The landlord owns the peasants but the peasants own the land" was a Russian saying from the days when land-owners measured their wealth in 'souls'; and the peasant seizure of the land preceded the Bolshevik seizure of power in 1917. David Mitrany recorded how

"The collapse of the old regime had been like a break in a dam, through which first a small trickle and then a rushing stream of spontaneous revolutionary action poured. The peasants began at once to take over forcibly large estates and forests, the number rising with every month from 17 in March, 204 in April, 259 in May, 577 in June, to 1,122 in July. It was estimated that in the first two years the peasants in thirty-six departments had taken over 86 per cent of the large estates and 80 per cent of their farm equipment; this increased their holding from 80 to 96.8 per cent of all usable land."[3]

In retrospect, the 1920s were the golden age of the Soviet 20th century, when "it was possible to find arrangements allowing peasant households to form a co-operative and yet keep their land, housing and equipment separately from each other and to make their own separate profits"[4] But in his very next sentence, the historian Robert Service, observes that "The idea of peasants taking most of their own decisions was anathema to Stalin." From the end of the decade, mass collectivisation destroyed the Russian peasantry. "The price was awful. Probably four to five million people perished in 1932-3 from 'de-kulakization' and from grain seizures."[5]

As citizens of the Soviet Union and its subsequent satellites were not allowed to discuss this terrible lesson, alternative approaches to food production had to emerge in the gaps that were subsequently allowed to emerge within the official policies. Eventually peasants were allowed to cultivate "private plots" and these became the salvation of Russia's food supply:

"In 1963, private plots covered about 44,000 square kilometres or some 4 per cent of all the arable land of the collective farms. From this 'private' land, however, comes about half of all the vegetables produced in the USSR, while 40 per cent of the cows and 30 per cent of the pigs in the country are on them."[6]

There are parallels between Winstanley's insistence that the woes of the English people stemmed from the Norman conquest and the claim that all land belonged to the King, and the insistence by millions of Soviet citizens that they had a right to colonise some minute patch of the land that they were told had been won back by the people. In England, as Oliver Rackham put it,

"William the Conquerer introduced the un-English doctrine that all land ultimately belongs to the Crown. It was part of the King's new, supreme, status that he had the right to keep deer on other people's land which lies at the heart of the Forest system."[7]

The same often-forgotten point was stressed by Simon Schama, noting that,

"Such 'forests' could be, and were, imposed on large areas of the English countryside, including the entire county of Essex, that were not wooded at all and which included tracts of pasture, meadow, cultivated farmland, and even towns."[8]

And just as the landless poor of mediaeval England sought out marginal patches of wasteland that they could colonise, so the economist Hugh Stretton reported from the Soviet Union in the 1970s that "Pathetically, Russian town dwellers go out and comb the countryside for patches of neglected land they can plant, visit, enjoy, 'make their own', however tenuously. Their masters, who own everything just as the masters did in Marx's day, discourage this petit-bourgeois practice."[9] But with the gradual collapse of the Soviet regime it was reported in 1985 that

"For the average Russian city dweller, it looks as if the first symbol of the Gorbachev era will be an allotment. The Politburo has authorised a series of measures designed to increase the number of private gardens — and these have already proved too few for the soaring demand... Once the plot has been dug, planted and harvested, the owner is allowed to put up a garden shed and, with a little creative interpretation of the rules, a shed can become a small dacha..."[10]

All the countries of Eastern Europe provided variations on the Soviet experience. Western visitors to the cities of Poland, Czechoslovakia, Hungary, Romania, Bulgaria and Yugoslavia would notice the landscape of gardens and dweller-built chalets along the routes from the airport to the city centre. Ian Hamilton reported that

> "The existence of peasant-owned land on the fringes of cities offers opportunities for piecemeal evolution — indeed 'overnight mushrooming' of 'wild settlements' as in Nowy Dwor and elsewhere outside Warsaw or in Kozarski Bok and Trnje on the margins of Zagreb..."[11]

Closer to home, the British planning system, built around the Town and Country Planning Acts passed by democratically elected parliaments and administered by democratically elected local authorities, has been far more effective in excluding the urban poor from the rural hinterland. The application of the legislation on planning, building and public health has ensured a bloodless elimination of any surviving peasantry from rural England. In Chapter 11 I quoted the industrial historian L.C.T. Rolt, who described in the 1970s the changes he had witnessed in the west of England, where cottagers became council house dwellers.[12]

The local gentry despised those raw new council houses, and made jokes about the inhabitants keeping coal in the bath. The tenants were thrilled to be offered not only a bathroom but a water-closet, and adequate damp-free rooms, offered by no previous village landlord. But under the Thatcher regime, not only were councils obliged to sell their houses, but they were prevented from spending the income on building more. This fact, together with the shift in attitudes which makes all new buildings (apart, thanks to the political influence of the agricultural lobby, from farm buildings) a blot on the landscape, has to be coupled with the fact that permission to build multiplies the value

171

of a rural site tenfold. The result is that the adult children of local families have little chance of housing themselves, and rent rooms in the nearest town, while the new occupants of those picturesque cottages are in the forefront of the village preservation society, since as Professor Gerald Wibberley used to explain, they want their particular village to remain exactly as it was on the day before they decided to move there.

In one of several reports, Mark Shucksmith has described the way in which rural Britain has been transformed into an exclusive countryside where only well-off people can afford to live. He observes that,

> "The studies suggest that progressive 'gentrification' of rural England will continue, as wealthier households outbid poorer groups for scarce housing, and 'social exclusion' thus becomes 'geographical exclusion'. Planning for and resourcing affordable housing provision is fundamental to sustaining rural communities and to the life-chances of many people."[13]

The effective challenge to the situation where only the affluent with their double garages and four-wheel-drive vehicles, can inhabit rural Britain has come, not from political movements, but from people with aspirations to feed themselves on a small patch of ground and warmly supporting the British government's commitment to sustainable development agreed at the Earth Summit at Rio in 1972. Simon Fairlie was one of a group of friends in the west of England who rented a house with a large garden on a country estate, but was evicted to make room for a golf course. After living in a van for two years, he joined another group and bought a smallholding with no house attached. They pitched seven tents and started cultivation. The result, he reported, was that "In the two years since we moved onto our land, we have been through almost the entire gamut of planning procedure: committee decision, enforcement order, stop notice, Article 4 application, Section 106 agreement, appeal, call in by the Secretary of State and statutory review in the High Court. "All this for seven tents!"[14]

Eventually, he and his friends won the right to stay, and similar settlements, like the bender community of King's Hill, also battled with the planning legislation, and likewise won permission to stay. Fairlie's case is interesting, not only as a precedent, but because it led to his very significant involvement in the debate on planning. His purpose has not been to demonise the planning machinery. He believes in it because he knows that without it, speculative developers would have completed the destruction of the countryside, subsidised for years to destroy woodlands, wetlands, hedges and wildlife. At the Town and Country Planning Summer School at Lancaster in 1993, Sir Richard Body, a farmer and then a Conservative Member of Parliament, had revealed that "the intensification of agriculture in the last 25 years has gone ahead faster and more furiously in the United Kingdom than in any other member state of the EC." He read to the assembled planners what he called "the woeful litany of statistics of the damage inflicted on the rural environment by government subsidies to farmers." These included:

— 130,000 miles (210,000 km) of hedgerows ripped up
— 40 per cent of our ancient woodlands gone
— seven million acres (2.8 million ha) of pasture-land ploughed up
— over 95 per cent of our wetlands drained
— 875 miles (1410 km) of stone wall destroyed
— 95 per cent of the downlands of Southern England gone
— 180,000 acres (73,000 ha) of moorland ploughed up

He went on to say that it infuriated participant observers like him, that having subsidised the owners of rural land to do all this damage in the name of increased food output, we are now "Paying the farmer to manage the countryside and thus protect the rural environment."[15]

173

In the last years of the last century changes in subsidy policy, arising from the embarrassment of European 'food mountains' reduced the incomes of rural land-owners, which had been inflated for decades, and brought the emergence of a 'rural lobby' claiming that the countryside was under threat from ignorant townsmen who failed to understand traditional rural ways. It was left to Peter Hall and the present writer to point to the evidence of official statistics that the quantity of land 'set aside' under European agricultural policy and handsomely subsidised for producing nothing, was three times the amount of land needed to accommodate all urban development predicted in Britain for the coming quarter century.[16]

The facts about rural Britain are a quiet testimony to the way in which the affluent, pleading the cause of countryside protection have sought to exclude the poor. The immense value of the campaigns associated with *The Land is Ours* has been that, virtually alone, they have re-opened discussion of the key issue of the right of all of us, just through having been born on this earth, to enjoy a right of access to our modest share of it. The Rural Planning Group of that campaign is known as 'Chapter 7'. This is because that section of the Agenda 21 agreement on 'Promoting sustainable human settlements' had a series of affirmations, the first of which explains that "the objective is to provide access to land for all households... through environmentally sound planning."

Chapter 7A of that document, stressing social justice, urged that "all countries should, as appropriate, support the shelter efforts of the urban and rural poor by adopting and/or adapting existing codes and regulations to facilitate their access to land finance and low cost building materials."

Chapter 7G is a reminder of the aims of those of the Arts and Crafts movement of a century earlier, like William Richard Lethaby, who wanted rural housing that would 'rise like a lark from the furrows'. For Chapter 7G declares that

"All countries should... strengthen the indigenous building materials industry, based, as much as possible, on inputs of locally available natural resources... promote the increased use of energy efficient designs and technologies and sustainable use of natural resources... promote the use of labour-intensive construction methods... develop policies and practices to reach the informal sector and self-help builders... discourage the use of construction materials and products that create pollution during their life cycle."[17]

The British government is committed to these aims through its predecessor's signature of the Rio Declaration of 1992, and this also involved commitment to the concept (in Chapter 7C) of "access to land for all households... through environmentally sound planning." There is little sign of the acceptance of these precepts in the Planning Policy Guidance Notes that flow from government to local planning authorities. There are signs, however, not that planning authorities are abandoning the profligate policies of the past, but that, with the added incentive of the incorporation into British law of the European Convention on Human Rights, they will be obliged to accommodate the planning system to those people supported by Chapter 7 — those "who sort out their own housing, in self-built houses, mobile homes, trucks, benders or sheds at no cost to the taxpayer more or less in defiance of the planning system."[18]

This recognition, when it comes, will be an ultimate gesture towards the centuries of cotters and squatters who housed themselves in the margins of history.

References

1. George Woodcock *Pierre-Joseph Proudhon: a biography*, London: Routledge & Kegan Paul 1956 p.45.
2. Christopher Hill (ed) *Gerrard Winstanley: the law of freedom and other writings*, Harmondsworth: Penguin Books 1973.

3.   David Mitrany *Marx Against the Peasant: a study in social dogmatism* (1951), New York: Collier Books 1961 pp. 80-81. For an anarchist account see Voline (V.M. Eichenbaum) *The Unknown Revolution*, London: Freedom Press 1955.

4.   Robert Service *A History of Twentieth-Century Russia*, London. Allen Lane 1997 p.183.

5.   *ibid* p.181.

6.   J.P. Cole *A Geography of the USSR*, Harmondsworth: Penguin Books 1967 p.167.

7.   Oliver Rackham *Trees and Woodland in the British Landscape*, London: J.M. Dent 1976 p.165.

8.   Simon Schama *Landscape and Memory*, London: Harper Collins 1995 p.144.

9.   Hugh Stretton *Capitalism, Socialism and the Environment*, Cambridge University Press 1976.

10. Martin Walker "The Seeds of a Revolution" *The Guardian* 14 May 1985, see also David Crouch & Colin Ward *The Allotment: its landscape and culture*, London: Faber & Faber 1988, Nottingham: Five Leaves Books.

11. Ian Hamilton "Spatial structure in East European cities" in F.E. French and Ian Hamilton *The Socialist City*, Chichester: John Wiley 1979.

12. L.C.T. Bolt *Landscape with Figures*, Stroud: Alan Sutton 1992.

13. Mark Shucksmith *Exclusive countryside? Social Inclusion and Regeneration in Rural Britain*, York: Joseph Rowntree Foundation 2000.

14. Simon Fairlie *Low Impact Development Planning and People in a Sustainable Countryside*, Oxfordshire: Jon Carpenter 1996, p.x.

15. Richard Body "Countryside Planning" in *Town & Country Planning Summer School, Lancaster: Report*, London: RTPI 1993 pp. 62-66.

16. Peter Hall & Colin Ward *Sociable Cities: the legacy of Ebenezer Howard*, Chichester: John Wiley 1998, pp. 107-108.

17. Rio Declaration, Agenda 21, cited in Simon Fairlie *Defining Rural Sustainability: fifteen criteria for sustainable developments in the countryside*, 1999 (From Chapter 7, The Potato Store, Flaxdrayton Farm, South Petherton, Somerset TA13)

18. Editorial in *Chapter 7 News* No 5, Autumn 2000, p.2.